Fluff Productions in association with Park Theatre presents

The World Premiere of

World Enough and Time

By Sarah Sigal

First Performance at Park Theatre, Wednesday 19th March 2014

Published by Playdead Press 2014

© Sarah Sigal 2014

Sarah Sigal has asserted her rights under the Copyright, Design and Patents Act, 1988, to be identified as the author of this work.

A CIP catalogue record for this book is available from the British Library.

ISBN 978-1-910067-09-3

Caution

All rights whatsoever in this play are strictly reserved and application for performance should be sought through the author before rehearsals begin. No performance may be given unless a license has been obtained.

This book is sold subject to the condition that it shall not by way of trade or otherwise, be lent, resold, hired out, or otherwise circulated without the publisher's prior consent in any form of binding or cover other than that in which it is published and without a similar condition including this condition being imposed on the subsequent purchaser.

Printed by BPUK

Playdead Press
www.playdeadpress.com

World Enough and Time

By Sarah Sigal

Cast in order of appearance

Celia/Anne	Jess Murphy
Lucy/Joan	Katie Bonna
Pamela	Rebecca Dunn
Meg/Katrina	Yvonne Riley
Bess/Tamara	Sarah Kameela Impey

The action takes place in London 2014, London 1936 and The West Country 1646

The Performance lasts approximately 1 hour and 40 minutes with a 15 minute interval.

Director	Justin Audibert
Designer	Lily Arnold
Lighting Designer	Joshua Pharo
Sound Designer	Mark Webber
Casting Director	Emily Jones
Production Manager	Timothy Peacock
Assistant Director	Rebecca Hill
Assistant Designer	Anna Reid
Stage Manager	Bethany Roberts
Assistant Producer	Miyuki Kasahara Fernandez

Fluff Productions

Artistic Directors
Rebecca Dunn
Emily Jones

Artistic Associates
Ailsa Ilott
Fiona Putnam

Founders
Charlotte Donnelly
Rebecca Dunn
Sarah Finigan
Clare Fraenkel
Emily Jones
Fiona Putnam
Sara Templeman

www.fluffproductions.co.uk
@WeAreFluff
Facebook: Fluff Productions

Fluff Productions are an all female theatre company dedicated to performing original and exciting new writing. Fluff was formed in 2004 by drama school graduates who quickly became aware of the lack of roles for women in theatre. The company aimed to redress the balance by producing newly written plays with all female casts.

Fluff has gone on to stage a number of phenomenally successful runs on the London and Edinburgh Fringe and on tour.

The double bill of *Snapshots*, a new play by Andrew Neil written for the company and Amanda Whittington's *Be My Baby*, both directed by Andrew Neil, set the precedent in 2005, playing to sell-out audiences and receiving rave reviews. Fluff went on to produce another of Andrew Neil's plays in 2005: *The Ark, the Bride and the Coffin*. Again written especially for the company, the play consolidated Fluff's reputation for producing inspiring, funny and innovative new writing for women.

In 2007 Fluff commissioned a new play by the Old Vic New Voices award nominee, Pericles Snowdon. The play *Bluebeard* was another huge success, receiving very favorable reviews and Time Out 'critics choice' award for two weeks running. Fluff then made their Edinburgh Festival debut in 2008 at The Underbelly, with *Lichentongue*, another new play by Pericles Snowdon. The show received outstanding reviews including 5 stars from Three Weeks.

Fluff then commissioned Sarah Sigal to write their next piece of new writing. Sarah wrote *Alice's Adventure in the New World*, which ran at The Old Red Lion in 2010 and toured the West Country in 2011, playing at venues including The Bike Shed Theatre, The Rhondo Theatre, Bath and The Cheltenham Everyman. Both runs were a huge success with more rave reviews. Fluff immediately got Sarah to work on another commission and began developing and works-shopping *World Enough and Time* with her in 2010.

Fluff recently held the inaugural season of Fluff Shorts. A new writing competition inviting writers to submit short plays on a chosen feminist issue. This season was in association with the No More Page 3 campaign and the three winning plays, *The Tea Party* by Katie Wimpenny, *Burst* by Ellie Rose and *Cock and Bull… The Rise of Excalibur* by Julie Balloo were all performed at Park Theatre in February 2014 to sell out audiences receiving much acclaim and a 5 star review from Female Arts

'*A spanking new five-star neighbourhood theatre*' Independent

Opened in May 2013, Park Theatre consists of two theatres - with 200 seats and 90 seats respectively - plus a dedicated community learning space, an all-day cafe-bar and ancillary facilities.

With a broad artistic policy encompassing both classics and new writing and an ambitious outreach programme, Park Theatre sits at the heart of its community.

'*A first-rate new theatre in north London*' Daily Telegraph

Park Theatre is a registered charity (number 1137223) and receives no public subsidy. Ticket sales alone are not enough to cover the running costs and it is only through your support that we can keep the theatre thriving. To donate please visit our website.

We rely on their tremendous support of our volunteer ushers to help staff the building - and enjoy including them in the Park family. If you're local and would like to volunteer as an usher then we'd love to hear from you. Please email our Operations Manager on operations@parktheatre.co.uk

If you're able to support us financially there are many ways from donating just £1 with your ticket booking to becoming a friend, naming a seat and even legacy giving - many of these come with an exciting array of benefits including priority booking, private tours and receptions. To discuss how you can support us please email our Development Director on development@parktheatre.co.uk

For more information and the latest on upcoming shows please visit the website: parktheatre.co.uk

We look forward to seeing you again soon.

Very best wishes,

Jez Bond
Artistic Director

For Park Theatre

Artistic Director	Jez Bond
Executive Director	John-Jackson Almond
Creative Director	Melli Bond
Development Director	Dorcas Morgan
Assistant to the Directors	Amy Lumsden
Finance Manager	Sharon Kwan
Operations Manager	Tom Kingdon
Box Office Supervisor / Duty Manager	Androulla Erotokritou
Host/Box Office Assistants	Raya Dibs, Hannah Halden, Amy Harper
Intern	Ivona Klemensova
President	Jeremy James
Trustees	Frances Carlisle
	Stephanie Dittmer
	Nick Frankfort
	Colin Hayfield
	Rachel Lewis
	Chris McGill
	Leah Schmidt
	Danielle Tarento

KATIE BONNA – Lucy/Joan

Katie graduated from Guildford School of Acting with the 2005 Graduate Spotlight Award for Achievement and the Max Adrian award for acting. She was nominated by The Stage for Best Actress in *Dirty Great Love Story* (which she co-wrote with Richard Marsh) in Edinburgh 2012. The show also won a Fringe First award and went on to run at SOHO Theatre and 59E59 Theaters in New York.

Theatre includes: *The London Merchant, He's Much To Blame* (Theatre Royal Bury St Edmunds); *Pygmalion, Up'n'Under, Relatively Speaking* (Chesterfield Pomegranate); *The Elephant Man* (Trafalgar Studios); *In The Club* (Hampstead Theatre tour); *Twelfth Night* (Red Handed Theatre); *Trojan Women* (Actor's of Dionysus).

Katie also works as a performance poet and has written and performed work for Nabokov, The Bush and the Roundhouse as well as at a huge number of spoken word nights and festivals.

Katie's one woman show, *The Celebrated Mrs Inchbald*, written for Theatre Royal Bury St Edmunds, toured to Texas in 2010. She co-founded Red Handed Theatre with Jessica Swale in 2006.

REBECCA DUNN - Pamela

Rebecca Trained at Drama Studio London

Theatre includes: *Be My Baby* (Old Red Lion); *Behind the Curtain* (The King's Head); *The Ark, The Bride and The Coffin* (Old Red Lion); *The Taming of The Shrew* and *King John* (Queen's Film Theatre, Belfast); *Bluebeard* (Old Red Lion – Critics Choice); *Lichentongue* (Underbelly, Edinburgh Festival); *Alice's Adventures in the New World* (Old Red Lion and UK Tour); *Away in a Banger* (The Courtyard Theatre); *Sorry Wrong Number* and *The Hitchhiker* (The Old Sorting Office); *Carbon Dating* (The Brockley Jack); and The *Tea Party* for Fluff Shorts: No More Page 3 (Park Theatre).

Film includes: *Loony in the Woods* (Ramar Productions); *Picture Perfect* (Miramotion Pictures); *Janice* (Low Fat Films).

SARAH KAMEELA IMPEY – Bess/Tamara

Sarah trained at Arts Educational.

Theatre includes: *A State of Nature* (Theatre Science); *A Clockwork Orange* (Fourth Monkey); *Arabian Nights, Hansel and Gretel* (Fairgame Theatre); *Women of Hope* (Tamasha/London Bus); National tour of *The Curiosity Shop* (Theatre Alibi); *Finding Noor* (Ankur Productions); *Cinderella a Fairytale* (The Tobacco Factory and Travelling light).

Sarah has also trained in basic aerial circus with Upswing and Circus Space, filmed shorts for Contiki travel in Vienna and Spain and was a dancer in the closing ceremony of the Olympics. She has just appeared in her first feature film

Halcyon Heights with Plug It In productions. The film was written for one of her best friends Thomas Hare an incredible actor and writer who passed away early 2013. A fund has been set up in his name 'The Tommy Vine Fund' and will provide financial and physical aid for emerging young artists creating their own work. Sarah would like to dedicated every performance from here on out to Tom.

JESS MURPHY – Celia/Anne

Theatre Includes: *Macbeth* (Globe Theatre); *People, Collaborators* (National Theatre); *War Horse* (New London Theatre); *Into Thy Hands* (Wilton's Music Hall); *The Hostage* (Southwark Playhouse); *The Unspeakable* (English Touring Theatre); *Brief Encounter* (Knee High, The Cinema Haymarket); *Bedroom Farce* (The Little Theatre); *Amadeus* (Wilton's Music Hall); *Perhaps Merely Quiet* (Icarus); *Blood Wedding* (Almeida); *Playing for Time* (Salisbury Playhouse).

Film includes: *Hereafter, Sweeney Todd*. Radio includes: *Collaborators*

YVONNE RILEY – Katrina/Meg

Yvonne Trained at Guildford School of Acting.

Theatre includes: *Calendar Girls* (West End); *Tales from Hollywood* (Donmar); *Beggar's Opera* (American Drama Group); *Greek, A Slight Joke* (Westcliff); *For Services Rendered* (Watermill); *Ruffian on the Stair* (Old Red Lion);

As You Like It (Kennington)
TV includes *Cherished* (BBC); *Government Inspector* (Ch4); *The Project* (BBC); *Inspector Lynley Mysteries* (BBC); *Queens Nose* (BBC); *London's Burning* (LWT); *The Bill* (Thames). Film includes *Ladybird Ladybird* dir. Ken Loach; *Loves Labours Lost* dir. Kenneth Branagh

SARAH SIGAL – Playwright

Sarah Sigal has a BA in English Literature and Theatre Arts from Gettysburg College and an MA in Writing for Performance from Goldsmiths College where she has recently completed a PhD on the role of the writer in collaborative theatre-making. She is a writer, dramaturg and director working in physical theatre, radio, devised work, live art, site-specific theatre, new writing and cabaret. Her most recent writing credits include *Alice's Adventures in the New World*, which was produced at the Old Red Lion in 2010 and went on national tour in 2011, and *The Odyssey*, which was produced at the Albany Theatre in 2012. Additionally, she has made work for the Shunt Vaults, the Union Theatre, the Cheltenham Everyman, the Arcola, the Edinburgh Festival, the Bike Shed, the Rondo, the Etcetera, the Bunker, the Rosemary Branch, Theatre503 and Horse Trade Theatre in NY. Sarah is currently working on a book about the role of the writer in collaborative theatre for Palgrave Macmillan. She is the Writer-in-Residence for Fluff Productions and the Creative Director of the performance-events company Hush-Hush Hoopla. Originally, from Chicago, she currently resides in London.

JUSTIN AUDIBERT – Director

Justin is a freelance theatre director and associate for Told By An Idiot, associate director for Red Ladder, and Artistic Associate for HighTide Festival Theatre. Recent directing credits include the Papatango New Writing Prize Winner

Unscorched by Luke Owen (Finborough Theatre); *The Fu Manchu Complex* (Oval House); *A Season In The Congo: Parallel Project* (Clare, Young Vic); *Wrong' Un* by Boff Whalley (Red Ladder); *Gruesome Playground Injuries* by Rajiv Joseph (Gate Theatre); *The Tempest* (RSC Shakespeare in a Suitcase); *Front* by Vickie Donoghue (Rada Festival); *Future Regrets* by Roz Wyllie (Live theatre / RSC); *Armley The Musical* by Boff Whalley (Interplay); and *Company Along The Mile* by Tom Bidwell (WYP / Arcola). As an Assistant Director he has worked with Greg Doran, Lucy Bailey, David Farr, Rachel Kavanaugh, Paul Hunter and Sarah Esdaile amongst others. He has directed at numerous drama schools including Drama Centre, GSA and ArtsEd and has worked for the Royal Shakespeare Company as an Education Associate Practitioner in the UK, the United States and Brazil. In 2012 he was the Acting Coach for the finalists of BBC 2's Shakespeare Off By Heart. He has been Resident Director at the National Theatre Studio, and was the recipient of the 2012 Leverhulme Award for Emerging Directors. Justin trained on the Birkbeck MFA in Theatre Directing.

LILY ARNOLD – Designer

Theatre and opera productions include, *Gruesome Playground Injuries* (Gate Theatre); *The Boss Of It All* (Assembly Edinburgh); *Yellow Face* (Park90 Theatre); *Happy New* (Trafalgar Studios); *King Lear* (RSC Touring); *I Cinna (the poet)* (RSC Swan Theatre); *A Midsummer Night's Dream* (Cambridge Arts Theatre); *The Taming Of the*

Shrew (RSC Swan Theatre); *Ahasverus* (RSC Hampstead Theatre Downstairs); *The Bullet* (RSC, Hampstead Theatre Downstairs); *Opera Scenes* (National Opera Studio); *Red Handed* (Robin Howard Dance Theatre).

Forthcoming productions include; *Peddling* (Hightide Festival); *Minotaur* (Polka Theatre)

JOSHUA PHARO – Lighting Designer

Joshua works as a Lighting and Projection Designer across theatre, dance, opera, music, film & art installation.
Recent credits: *Thumeblina* Dancing Brick (LD); *Cheese [a play]* fanSHEN (LD), *Pelleas & Melisande* The Arcola (LD), *Grounded* Gate Theatre (ALD); *The Collision of Things* Move to Stand (LD); *The Match Girls* Red Ladder (LD/PD); *Fox Solo* Foxy & Husk (LD); *Souvenir* Dead Centre (LD); *Sour Lips* Paper Tiger (LD/PD); *Faust* Dumbwise (LD); *Trojan Women* Gate Theatre (ALD); *Kreutzer Sonata* Gate Theatre / La Mama NYC (ALD); *Revolutions in Costume* London College Fashion (LD); *Purge* Arcola (LD).
Joshua is an Associate Artist of Ovalhouse Theatre for 2014.

MARK WEBBER – Sound Designer

Mark is a freelance Sound and Lighting Designer /Technician, Musical Director and a composer of Musical Theatre. He is also an Associate Sound Designer of Outfox Productions.

Previous sound design includes *The Effect of Gamma Rays on Man-in-the-Moon Marigolds*, *Rope* and *Carbon Dating* (Outfox Productions); *No Rhyme* (Jack Studio Theatre , Brockley); *On Beauty* (Absent Theatre); Lighting designs include *World Enough and Time* (Fluff Productions, Dalston Bunker); *4:48 Psychosis* (The London Theatre New Cross); *The Drowsy Chaperone* and *The Caucasian Chalk Circle (*Stanwix Arts Theatre) along with a large number of original works. Mark has also devised and designed for many shows during his MA in Performing Arts at Cumbria Institute of the Arts including *Blood on the Stars and Stripes* (Bad Wednesday Productions); *Due Process* and *Saving Grace* (www.productions).

Other credits include Musical Director for *Corpus Christi* (The Space, Isle of Dogs), *Joseph and the Amazing Technicolor Dreamcoat (*Palace Theatre, Redditch); *Hair*, *Little Women: The Broadway Musical* and *Bright Lights, Big City* (University of Cumbria); *The Last Five Years* (Hallmark Hotel, Carlisle); Composer for the musicals *If I Told You*, *1 in 3* and *Your Five Minute Call* (Webcam Productions). Mark was recently Technician/Re-lighter for the nationwide debut tour of the one-woman play *Floating (*Lives of Others Theatre Company).

EMILY JONES – Casting Director

Emily is resident casting director of Fluff productions. Her Theatre casting credits include *Unscorched* (Papatango at the Finborough), *The Keepers of Infinite Space* (Park Theatre), *As You Like It*, *Richard III* (Changeling Theatre),

World Enough and Time (Fluff Productions). Film credits include *Limbo* (JenX Films), *Ibiza Undead* (Temple Heart Films). She has assisted Ginny Schiller for the past year on over 20 productions, including *1984* for Headlong, *Relative Values* for The Theatre Royal Bath and *Scenes from a Marriage* at the St James, both directed by Trevor Nunn, *A Day in the Death of Joe Egg* and *Ghosts* at the Rose Theatre Kingston, and *Pride & Prejudice* at Regent's Park.

TIMOTHY PEACOCK – Production Manager

Tim Peacock is a graduate of the Guildhall School of Music & Drama's Stage Management & Technical Theatre course where he specialised in Production Management. Tim has worked on productions ranging from Opera, to site-specific children's theatre, to Musicals and with companies such as The National Theatre, The Royal Albert Hall and Punchdrunk. Tim also works as an AutoCAD draughtsman for various Theatres and Designers around the UK.

Theatre includes: *Under the Eiderdown* (Punchdrunk Enrichment), *Unscorched* (Papatango), *My Fair Lady & Anything Goes* (Kilworth House Theatre), *Story Balloonists – Dalston Land of Kids* (Punchdrunk Enrichment), *Too Hot to Handel* (Armonico Consort), *The Imperfect Pearl* (Whitehouse Productions), *Falstaff* (Opera Berbiguieres)

As Draughtsman: 3D Venue Drawings (Kilworth House Theatre), Performer Flying System (Robbie Williams – Take the Crown Tour 2013), Milton Court Concert Hall,

Theatre & Studio (Venue Drawings - GSMD), *The Village Bike* (Sheffield Crucible), *Gravity* (Birmingham Rep - The MAC), *Twelfth Night & Nicholas Nickleby Pt. 1 & 2* (Silk Street Theatre)

REBECCA HILL – Assistant Director

Rebecca is a director and playwright, co-director of Unbound Productions and an Associate Director of Little Pieces Of Gold. She has assistant directed and worked as Dramaturg with Lazarus Theatre Company and was Assistant Director to David Mercatali on the UK Tour and London Return of Philip Ridley's *Tender Napalm* (venues including Leicester Curve, York Theatre Royal, Hull Truck and Southwark Playhouse). Directing credits include *Travesti* (Etcetera Theatre, and Lost Theatre, 5 minute festival finalist), *Two Sisters* (Southwark Playhouse), *One Time Thing* (Park Theatre) and *Half-Way* (Ovalhouse Theatre).

ANNA REID – Assistant Designer

Anna is a set and costume designer based in London. Past credits include: *Macbeth* (Cambridge American Stage Tour); *More* (The Corpus Playrooms); *As You Like It* (C Venues Chambers Street, Edinburgh); *The Spanish Tragedy* (King's College Chapel, Cambridge); *The Other Line* (ADC Theatre, Cambridge). Assistant Designer credits: *A Midsummer Night's Dream* (Cambridge Arts Theatre) *Gruesome Playground Injuries* (The Gate Theatre), *The Fu Manchu*

Complex (Ovalhouse Theatre).

BETHANY ROBERTS – Stage Manager

Bethany is in her 3rd year at Central School of Speech and Drama studying Stage Management. She has mainly worked on productions within the University such as *Too Clever by Half* - a touring show, *Absolute Hell* and also on *Arabian Nights* at The Minack Theatre in Cornwall. Most recently she was Assistant Stage Manager on *The Fu Manchu Complex* at The Ovalhouse.

MIYUKI KASAHARA FERNANDEZ – Assistant Producer

Miyuki Kasahara is a theatre producer, dancer and choreographer. Born in Santo Domingo (Dominican Republic) she began performing as part of the Anna Pavlova Ballet Academy and in the annual Christmas Musical at the Jesus Maestro Church since 2009. She has been part of several other musical and performance productions as a dancer, choreographer and actress and has also been part of the production team for shows such as *Virtus Belum* (2010); *Memories* (2011); *Amazing Classics* (2011, 2012); and *Styles* (2012, 2013). From 2011 to 2013 she directed and produced the Annual Class Presentation at Loyola School. In April 2013 Miyuki graduated from the Technological Institute of Santo Domingo with a Bachelor's Degree in Marketing. She is currently undertaking a Master's Degree in Creative Producing for Theatre and Live Performance at Birkbeck, University of London.

Production acknowledgments:

An earlier draft of the play was performed as part of development at The Dalston Bunker in 2013

Directed by Helen Tennison

Cast: Morag Cross, Rebecca Dunn, Clare Fraenkel, Alexa Matthews, Holly McLay, Fiona Putnam, Yvonne Riley
Creatives: Harry Christopher, Zoe Dowler, Hannah Mills, Alex Scott, Jen Skivens, Hannah Spearing, Mark Webber,

Actors and creatives that contributed to development of the piece: Henry Evertett, Ailsa Ilott, Madeline Knight, Krupa Pattani, Linda Campbell

Rehearsal Space: Make Believe Arts
Production Photography: Karla Gowlett
Image: Lily Arnold
Graphic design: Terry Bright

Special thanks to: Kay Dunn, Robin Dunn, Richard Fry, Diane Bright, Brian Jones, Edward Jones, Pamela Jones, Nicola Cousins, Kilworth House Theatre, Matthew McCooey and JenX Films.

World Enough and Time

1: 2012

Celia – 34 (middle/upper-class English accent)

Lucy – early 30s (middle-class English accent, possibly regional)

Katrina –60-70s (upper-class English accent)

Tamara – 20-30s (affected, 'poshed-up' English accent)

2: 1936

Pamela – early 30s (clipped, upper-class, early-20th century English accent)

3: 1646

Anne – 30s (West Country accent)

Bess – 20s (West Country accent)

Meg – 40-50s (West Country accent)

Joan – 30-40s (West Country accent)

1

2014. London. Celia's house in Richmond. Lucy has couple of bags and a backpack with her.

CELIA: We're finally building that extension, so there will be paint fumes and workmen coming in and out...

LUCY: I'm hoping it will only be a couple of weeks, until I get back on my feet. It's just that you're the only person I know with a spare room.

CELIA: Don't worry, it won't be a problem. It's nice to see you, Lucy. It's been absolutely ages.

LUCY: It's been a long time. Thanks for putting me up, Celia.

CELIA: Really—don't worry. Terrible, having to deal with flatmates and house-shares and things. At our age. Do you remember Poppy, that flatmate I had just after unie?

LUCY: The one who left food everywhere?

CELIA: Food, clothes, cigarettes...dishes in the sink.

LUCY: You hated her. And she had that boyfriend...

CELIA: Étienne. He was French.

LUCY: Étienne! He was always playing the guitar in your front room.

CELIA: They were both dreadful, but I couldn't get rid of them because Poppy was India's friend from school.

Lucy looks around.

LUCY: You have such a lovely house. And a really amazing view of the park.

CELIA: This place was in a state when we bought it—otherwise we never would have been able to afford it. I can't imagine having to live with strangers again. It's too bad you can't afford to strike out on your own.

LUCY: How's Georgina? How old is she now?

CELIA: She's seven and growing like a weed. The nanny's taken her to her Mandarin lesson. They say it's good to start them early, especially with languages.

LUCY: How's Jeremy?

CELIA: Busy. He seems to be away for work more than ever. Hong Kong, at the moment. We're like ships passing in the night sometimes. We're lucky we have Magda. She's so good with the Georgina. I can't tell you how many nannies we've been through. Georgie's been acting up lately, being difficult to handle. We don't really know why. You look great, by the way.

LUCY: Really? Thanks.

CELIA: Have you dyed your hair or something?

LUCY: No.

CELIA: Well, you look fantastic.

LUCY: Thanks, Celia. I saw that you wrote a book.

CELIA: It's been really exciting, actually. I never thought I'd write a book in my life, but I was writing these memos and someone suggested it to me and before I knew it, I had an editor and a publicist and all these speaking engagements.

LUCY: That's great. Congratulations.

CELIA: Still working the same bloody hours though.

LUCY: I've been working on a book too.

CELIA: I thought you were teaching.

Celia's phone rings.

CELIA: Sorry, hold on a minute. It's work. *Celia picks up.* Hi, Paul. No, I haven't read the new email from Brian. Well, it is a Saturday. Yes, I know *you're* in the office. You're paid to be in the office on weekends. *Pause.* Well, when you're the COO you too can occasionally have the odd weekend off. *Pause.* What's he worried about now? Has he seen the new budget? *To Lucy.* Sorry! Be right back... Sorry, Paul—what?

Celia exits to the kitchen. Lucy sits alone in Celia's living room. She's tired so she lies down. Celia re-enters after a period of time. She has a bottle of wine and two glasses.

CELIA: God, sorry about that. Listen, I thought this called for some vino.

Celia pours two glasses. Lucy just looks at her glass.

LUCY: I stopped drinking a little while ago.

CELIA: You've stopped drinking? Surely not!

LUCY: I've been going to AA meetings.

CELIA: But you're not an alcoholic.

LUCY: Celia, you haven't seen me in a while. I was drinking too much.

CELIA: But surely—

LUCY: The thing is, I lost my job.

CELIA: God, I'm sorry to hear it.

LUCY: The workload was really heavy, with all the teaching and no time to prep. I started to dread going in to school. I kept having nightmares about falling.

CELIA: That's just terrible. But it was an inner-city comp. That was always going to be a struggle.

LUCY: I wanted to teach somewhere where I could make a difference.

CELIA: Lucy, you can make a difference anywhere.

LUCY: I don't know about that. *Pause.* I'm kind of relieved actually. I've had more time to work on my novel.

CELIA: You're writing a novel?

LUCY: I've been working on it for years, off and on.

CELIA: What's it about?

LUCY: Addiction, actually.

CELIA: Sounds very intense.

Lucy takes an enormous, well-worn notebook out of her bag.

CELIA: You don't *hand-write* everything, do you?

LUCY: I know it's old-fashioned but I feel like I have more of a connection with what I'm writing. It feels more...I don't know...emotional.

CELIA: I'm a bit jealous, to be honest. I'd love to be able to write a novel.

LUCY: You just wrote a book.

CELIA: It would be nice to write fiction. Something enjoyable. Live somewhere in the country or sit on a beach and write all day.

LUCY: Do you think that's something you could aim for?

CELIA: *Laughs.* Not with my job. And Jeremy and Georgina. Too many balls in the air. Maybe when I'm retired. *Pause.* I didn't know you were going through such a hard time, Lucy.

LUCY: I mean, it's been pretty grim but since I've started going to meetings, I've been feeling better.

CELIA: Now you can make a fresh start.

LUCY: Yeah… I'm a little worried about money now. It's been really hard to find a job.

CELIA: Maybe your CV needs going over. You should get a new suit. For interviews. You need to pick yourself up and start thinking positively. I'm going to give you a copy of my book. I actually think you might find it interesting. It's about personal career empowerment. Women need to take control of their own destinies. Learn how to fulfil their potential. They just need to believe in themselves and aim higher. I think we undermine ourselves before we even begin. I mean, we as women are naturally team players, but we need to learn to be more driven in the workplace. More goal-orientated. Ambitious. Aggressive.

LUCY: You sound like a football manager.

CELIA: I did research sports psychology when I was writing the book, actually. That was Jeremy's idea.

LUCY: That's a very corporate brand of feminism.

CELIA: I think feminism is too sharp a term. It's become too loaded, too hostile. Alienating. The whole 'are you a feminist thing' is a trap.

LUCY: A trap? Do you really think that?

CELIA: Absolutely. I want to start a conversation about what we *can* do as women, as opposed to what we *can't* do. For ourselves. I'm not interested in talking about glass ceilings and pay discrepancies and men being better than women or women being better than men. Women just need to get their noses to the grindstone. We need to spend less time complaining and second-guessing ourselves and get to work. I was interviewing a girl for a position at my company and she said, I'm worried about childcare. I said, well how old are your children? She said, I don't have any yet, but I'm planning on having children. I asked her how long she's been married. She said she wasn't married. The poor girl didn't even have a boyfriend! Women stop themselves from achieving because they worry too much about whether they'll be able to do it or not. We undersell ourselves. I get up at five am every morning, and that's after going to bed around one. I hardly get more than four or five hours of sleep, but I still come into work every morning, and I serve on the boards of three different companies and two charities. I still manage to raise my daughter, even if I hardly ever see her. I was back in the office within a week after Georgie was born. Why can't women just get to work and stop whingeing? I just think we have to feel empowered to help ourselves.

2

1936. London.

PAMELA: Going on holiday for a few weeks is all well and good, but I can't really imagine living anywhere but London. My sister Charlotte and her husband Peter are constantly abroad. They may as well not have bothered to have children at all—it isn't as if they ever see them. Christopher and Alexandra were bundled off to school at the earliest opportunity, and are occasionally sent for to someplace like Monaco or Persia or goodness-knows-where for the holidays. My husband Francis is disapproving. He says it is no way to raise a child. We hardly hear from Charlotte and Peter these days. Just a letter or a postcard now and then. Hello from Mongolia—we had the most wonderful yak soup, which was just delicious after a long hike in the mountains! California is so sunny and warm—Peter's friend who makes darling little films introduced us to Clark Gable! Italy is gorgeous this time of year—the wine is fantastic, the tomatoes are in season and we've been listening to Il Duce on the wireless! Who Il Duce is, I've no idea. Probably an opera singer or something.

Francis and I don't have any children of our own. I suspect Francis is still hopeful, but I'm terribly busy. I write a fashion column for The Times, you see. No one seems to have the foresight that I do when it comes to haute couture, so it really is crucial that I am out and about, keeping in touch with what women are wearing. Luncheons, cocktail parties, balls. To be perfectly frank, I'm really not sure that

I'm cut out for pregnancy and child-rearing. One does hear such awful things from other women about the period when one is expecting. Being ill in the morning. How one's feet grow a whole shoe size. Lugging one's own body around as if one were carrying a steamer trunk. Some women never manage to regain the figure they had before the pregnancy. They just balloon up and settle comfortably into domestic life. When my sister had Christopher, her eldest, she managed to retain that teeny-tiny figure of hers. She was one of those women who hardly showed until she was practically due. But when she had Alexandra, she was an absolute whale. She had been so smug, it was downright exciting to see her get so fat the second time round.

3

1646. The West Country. Brookfield House. Anne is practicing a speech. She is watched by her servants Bess and Meg.

ANNE: Men and women of Little Brideford, I thank you for permitting me to address you. Upon my faith and honour, I accept I am merely a woman and a poor substitute for my late husband, Sir William More, but in these troubled times, I beseech you to...I beseech you...hm...

Anne crosses things off and writes corrections.

ANNE: I would like to begin with a line from the poet John Donne...

Anne hesitates. She scribbles a correction on a piece of paper and starts over.

ANNE: I would like to begin by saying...

She takes a deep breath.

ANNE: You have endured war and poverty, famine and disease these last four years and you have born your crosses with great strength and courage. You have suffered the loss of sons, husbands, fathers and brothers on the battlefield. You have born your babes and raised your children alone. There have been rumours about His Majesty the King and about his troops...that Cromwell's army is on the march and moving in the direction of our village. I cannot confirm or deny whether these rumours are true because I do not know. What I do know is that you are afraid. I have suffered along with each and every one of you, but now we must take control of our destiny. So I propose a vote. Other villages in the county of Somerset have banded together to protect themselves from the Roundheads. Indeed, from both armies. To protect each other and to protect peace. If there was an agreement among us that we wanted to join with neighbouring towns to protect ourselves and our families, this might be possible. To wit, I propose that we put it to a vote.

MEG: A vote, ma'am?

ANNE: Yes, a vote.

BESS: Meg, she weren't finished.

MEG: You think folk'll want to vote? In the open air, seen by all their neighbours?

ANNE: Perhaps it should be arranged that folk vote in private.

MEG: How would they do that?

ANNE: They could write down which action they would prefer to vote for.

MEG: But most folk can't read nor write.

BESS: Why don't you make the decision, ma'am? For all of us.

ANNE: I want the people in this village to have a say in actions that will affect their lives.

MEG: Only five men left in the village to vote. Six if you count Sam, the baker's son, and he's a bit wrong in the head.

ANNE: I mean for the women to vote as well.

MEG: The women?

ANNE: It's time we too had a say. After all, only six men remain in the village.

BESS: T'was a fine speech, m'lady.

ANNE: But...will they suffer a woman to speak? And will they listen?

MEG: Ye've been good to the people in this parish through the war. Ye opened up yer granaries when Parliament hiked up them grain prices. Ye let them graze their sheep 'n cows on yer land when others enclosed the commons.

BESS: Now the King's took flight ain't no one else to turn to.

MEG: Abandoned by our own King Charlie, after all we done fer 'im.

ANNE: We mustn't speak like that, Meg.

BESS: He could return yet. Prolly gatherin' his troops, like. Layin' in wait.

MEG: Ain't been no news about him in some time. Don't think no one knows where he is. Scotland? France?

ANNE: The news has been so inconstant these past few months.

MEG: Could be captured by now.

BESS: Blessed Jesus... If his Majesty is captured...what then? Is the war lost?

ANNE: I can hardly bear to think on it, Bess.

BESS: They can't, ma'am. They can't lose.

ANNE: It seems anything is possible these days.

BESS: If His Majesty's army were to fall to the Roundheads... What would happen to Little Brideford? To Brookfield House?

ANNE: I don't know.

MEG: Folk will seek your guidance, as they did his lordship's, and your father's before him.

We hear a knock at the door. Bess opens in. Joan enters. She looks haggard and has been travelling. She has a frightened, haunted look in her eye.

JOAN: Beggin' your pardon, ma'am.

MEG: We ain't got room in the house, but you can sleep in the stables.

JOAN: It's Joan...Joan Rainesford.

ANNE: Joan. My goodness. Please, come in.

JOAN: Your ladyship?

ANNE: You'd hardly recognize me these days. As you can see, the war has much reduced our circumstances.

Joan enters, tentatively. She is amazed at Lady Anne's appearance.

JOAN: God bless and keep you, ma'am.

ANNE: And you, Joan. We've not seen you these many years.

JOAN: Been travelling. Doin' a bit of this an' a bit of tha'. Just enough to keep body an' soul together.

ANNE: Please. Sit. Would you like something to eat?

JOAN: Very kind of you, m'lady.

ANNE: Bess, would you please get this woman something from the larder.

BESS: But, m'lady...

ANNE: There must be *something*, Bess.

JOAN: How is his lordship?

ANNE: His lordship has been dead these past two years. Killed in the fighting.

JOAN: I'm sorry, m'lady. Bless his soul...

ANNE: You don't look well, Joan.

JOAN: It's sleepin' rough that does it, I'll warrant.

ANNE: How have you been keeping?

JOAN: Winter's cruel on a body. I wouldn't dare ask, m'lady, but...times is hard...with the war... You got anywhere for me to stay? Just for a spell. I'll work. I'm a good worker.

Bess starts to exit but Meg takes her aside. She whispers to her so that Joan and Lady Anne can't hear them.

MEG: Don't you know who that is?

BESS: No.

MEG: That's Mad Joan.

BESS: Mad Joan? The one wot they put in the...the...

MEG: Scold's Bridle. Ain't seen her in nigh on seven year now. What's her ladyship doin', takin' her in?

BESS: Christian charity, ain't it?

MEG: She can't shelter that woman.

BESS: Why not?

MEG: We'll all be done for witchcraft.

Bess exits, frightened.

ANNE: You kept away for so long, Joan.

JOAN: There's some here who'd have me hanged. So I took to the roads. Disappeared.

ANNE: I didn't know.

JOAN: But I come back 'cause the Puritans, they sees witches everywhere. Any lone woman who ain't known to a parish or a village is suspect. Can't scarcely spend a night anywhere without folk askin', Mother, where you from? Askin', Mother, why ain't you home with yer man 'n yer babies? I do odd jobs here 'n there but soon as there's suspicion, I disappear. They say that Cromwell has a man wot follows his armies wherever he goes. Cleansing the villages of Papists 'n witches. I ain't got nowhere else to go, my lady.

4

2014. London. Celia's flat. Celia's mother Katrina is helping Celia redecorate her drawing room. She sits with a pile of fabric swatches and paint samples, comparing and contrasting how different combinations would look. Celia is working on her laptop. Lucy is reading.

KATRINA: Celia darling, have you put on weight? Lucy, do you think Celia's put on weight?

LUCY: I—

KATRINA: Do you think you're pregnant again?

CELIA: It's highly unlikely.

KATRINA: Don't you think Georgina would like a little brother or sister? Wouldn't it be fun? I could do up the nursery again! Speaking of which, have you been taking her to church? Because if you left her with your father and me for a weekend or two...

CELIA: Mummy...

KATRINA: I know you and Jeremy are so busy. The fresh air is good for her. She just loves it in the country. She's far too cosseted here in London. She should be allowed more freedom.

CELIA: Not in London, Mummy. Not at her age. You have to watch her all the time.

KATRINA: Lucy, being a teacher you must be naturally good with children. Celia had to learn, you see.

Celia glares at her mother.

LUCY: I taught English in a secondary school. They were teenagers.

KATRINA: Teenagers...what a nightmare. The drugs, the drinking. In my day, it was considered quite unattractive to drink so heavily at such a young age. At least for girls. And the violence! Gangs and things like that. Do you know that Celia was chased in the park the other week whilst she was out jogging? A couple of teenagers trying to frighten her. And in this neighbourhood! They must have come from the estate down the road. Where are their parents, I wonder?

LUCY: Working, I assume.

KATRINA: These people need to understand that there are consequences to their actions. This government is too soft on criminals. Criminals and people looking for handouts. This country has changed so much since I was your age, it's unrecognisable. I personally think bringing back national service would solve a lot of problems. It would provide training, an education, instil some discipline. My father went to Sandhurst and it was the making of him. Do you want to have children, Lucy?

LUCY: I don't know if I'll be able to.

KATRINA: You should see a doctor. There are all sorts of things they can do these days with IVF.

LUCY: I mean, I don't know if I'll be able to...*afford* to have children.

KATRINA: I didn't mean you should have to do it all on your own! Make sure you marry well if you're going bother to do it at all, that's what my mother always said. Celia, who can we introduce Lucy to? Geraldine and Richard Holinsbrook's son Edward is recently divorced, I hear. Very good-looking boy. Used to play rugby. He might like Lucy—she's such a good-looking girl.

CELIA: Ed Holinsbrook is a bore.

KATRINA: Didn't you go out with him for a while when you were a teenager, Celia?

CELIA: No, that was India.

KATRINA: Of course you could always freeze your eggs. They do that nowadays.

CELIA: Mummy, Lucy doesn't need to freeze her eggs.

KATRINA: They say that after thirty-five, a woman's chances of having a Down's Syndrome baby increase exponentially.

Katrina holds up fabric swatches for Celia.

KATRINA: What do you think of these?

CELIA: Mummy, I told you...I can get a decorator in to do that.

KATRINA: Do you always work after dinner?

CELIA: Yes. Otherwise I wouldn't be coming home until practically midnight. And now with the book tour coming up...

KATRINA: Such uncivilised hours. This email business and everyone being on their Blackberrys and their i-whatsits all the time.

Celia looks at her phone.

CELIA: Speaking of which, it looks like Jeremy's working late. Again.

KATRINA: What a shame. Is everything all right with the two of you, darling?

CELIA: Yes, of course. He's just working.

LUCY: Sorry, Celia, he mentioned to me this morning on his way out that he'd probably be working late tonight and not to include him in dinner plans.

Katrina turns to Lucy, who is reading, off to the side.

KATRINA: Lucy, what do you think? Which do you prefer?

Katrina holds up the fabric swatches for inspection.

CELIA: Mum, by all means, carry on with what you're doing if it makes you happy, but I have work to do and Lucy is applying for jobs.

KATRINA: How tedious. It's just hideous out there, isn't it? I don't know how anyone does it these days. I think the most important thing is to have a very good suit. Start by looking the part. Can't you help her get something, darling? You know so many people. I think everyone needs a little help sometimes. I'm on the board of the Westminster School—that's where Celia and her brother and sister went. I could have a word with the headmaster for you.

LUCY: I appreciate the offer, but... I was teaching at a state school.

KATRINA: Yes. Exactly. This will be a step up in your career.

LUCY: I just think...I mean, I know it's an excellent school but...I feel that if everyone sent their children to the same kind of schools...everyone would be better off.

Silence.

KATRINA: Lucy, everyone's an idealist before they have children of their own. When you have children, you will very likely want the best for them too. And then I think you'll change your mind.

Celia's phone rings.

CELIA: Hi, Magda. What's wrong? *Pause.* Oh, good. Nothing's wrong. You always seem to call when something's wrong. Is it Georgie again? *Pause.* I know, I'm sorry. It's not very fair to you, is it? Look, we'll compensate you with time and a half for the overtime hours, of course. *Pause.* I know she can be a handful but you've been so good with her! *Pause.* Magda, I really hope we can—*Pause.* Why? For how long? *Pause.* Yes, yes fine. I can't stop you, can I? *Pause.* Yes. Bye.

Celia hangs up.

KATRINA: Not another nanny, darling?

CELIA: Christ, we've been through about four in the last three years. I just don't understand it. They always say Georgie's difficult but I've never seen it. Her excuse was my schedule is too irregular and something about going back to Poland. I can't always understand her English.

KATRINA: Oh, what a bother! I told you not to go through that agency. Those Eastern-European girls are so unreliable. All they want to do is go home to their families.

CELIA: Well, that's the last one I'm using from them. It's just a nightmare. God, what am I going to do now?

Celia looks at Lucy.

CELIA: Lucy...when you were doing your teacher training, you used to nanny, didn't you?

LUCY: Yeah...

CELIA: I really hate to ask you this, and please don't say yes unless you feel comfortable doing it, but Georgina really seems to like you. Just for a little while, just until I find someone else...would you mind giving me a hand with her? It would be such a help.

LUCY: I'm just a bit worried that I won't have enough time to look for jobs. And I'm so close to finishing my book.

CELIA: Of course. And I don't want to put any pressure on you at all.

LUCY: Well...ok. I mean, of course. It's not a problem.

CELIA: Are you sure? You don't mind?

LUCY: It's fine.

CELIA: You're a lifesaver, Lucy. And if you let me have a look at your work—I mean, whenever you're ready, not that I'm an expert—I could always show it to my editor. She might know someone who might be interested in your book.

LUCY: Really?

CELIA: As a thank you. But of course I would anyway, you know. Anything to help.

5

1936. London.

PAMELA: I usually avoid meetings at the paper like the plague, but despite my protestations, Geoffrey Dawson—he's the editor-in-chief—insisted I come to this week's meeting. And I didn't really understand why at first, as all anyone seemed to want to talk about was Germany. I know Mr. Hitler's done rather a lot for the Germans, getting them back on their feet. The economy. That sort of thing. But it does seem a bit over the top. The saluting and the marching. The leather. And that curious little moustache. Like the bristles on a toothbrush. (One rather hopes that's a look that won't catch on.)

Francis says the man's a thug and not to be trusted—probably no better than Stalin. Do you think it will come to that? I said. A choice between the Fascists and the Communists? No one's really trusted the Boche since the Great War, but good lord...the thought of being overrun with wild-eyed Bolsheviks. Galloping through the streets. Kidnapping the Royal Family. Marching into the House of Lords and shooting everyone. Francis would be the first to go—he can get awfully shouty when he's cross. I'd be made to drive a bus. Wear dowdy clothes. Cut my hair short. We might even be forced to flee the country in the dead of night. The horror. Short hair really doesn't suit me.

Dawson rabbitted on about Hitler's great economic vision for Germany. David Stern, a funny little man who has an opinions column, said we're ignoring the terrible laws he's imposing on his own people and turning a blind eye to what he's going to do to Europe. He said the Rhineland (wherever that is) is only the beginning. Dawson said, well David, someone needs to take the reins in Europe before we have another crash. And then of course whatever is going on in Spain had to be discussed. Henry Rake, one of our editors, started to sniffle, tearfully explaining his son had gone to fight in Spain. It did go on for such a long time and no one made tea, which I found very insensitive indeed. I don't understand how people can get so worked up about things going on in other people's countries. I leave politics to the politicians.

I may have fallen asleep for a moment. I awoke with a start when Dawson called from the end of the table, Pamela! Pamela, are you with us? Everyone was staring at me. I was just resting my eyes, I replied, cool as a cucumber. Your assignment, Pamela, he said, will be a feature called, 'A Week with Wallis'. Who's Wallis? I asked. Wallis Simpson, Dawson replied. The American favourite of the King. Dawson explained that there was a gentleman's agreement on a blackout regarding coverage of the situation, as Mrs. Simpson was a soon-to-be divorced American and not an appropriate royal companion. Doris, Dawson's secretary, snorted loudly, muttering, companion my foot...if she's only the King's *companion*, then I'm the Queen of Sheba. A few people tittered. Dawson glared and they fell silent. Apparently, this Simpson Woman was known to be very chic. So as long as I did not mention the King and simply wrote about what the woman wore, we would be able to feed people's interests without breaking any confidences. No politics, just fashion. Suits me, I said.

6

1646. Brookfield House. Meg is sitting by the hearth in the kitchen, smoking a pipe. Lady Anne is in the middle of teaching her to read by using 'To His Coy Mistress' by Andrew Marvell.

MEG: Had we but...world...eee...eeen...

ANNE: Enough.

MEG: Enough. And time. *Pause.* Had we but world...enough...and time. This...coy...coyness... *Pause.* What's coy-ness, ma'am?

ANNE: To be shy or reserved. Here, Marvell means...well...read on...

MEG: This coy-ness, lady, were no crime. We would sit...down...and think...which way to walk...and pass our long...love's day.

Meg stops. She puffs on her pipe and looks into the fire.

MEG: Flattery and fornication. Had we but world enough and time...this coy-ness, lady, were no crime. In other words, hurry up 'n hitch up yer skirts, lass. Had we but world enough and time... If we had all the time in the world I'd bring you roses and lay them at yer feet. And nowt else once you're with child... Them poets wrote them poems to get some young lass to lay with 'em. It ain't the way folk live truly. Weren't the way me husband were with me. Tom would give me a good hiding sooner 'n he'd read poetry to me, not that he could read. Pity women don't write poems 'n books. Be a damn sight different, I'd wager.

Silence.

ANNE: Shall we carry on?

MEG: If it please you, ma'am. But I can figure how it ends without reading it. They tell you their love is constant and one day you wake up alone.

ANNE: Not all men are rogues and scoundrels.

MEG: They quit us all the same.

ANNE: Their devotion was of a different kind. William said if the Roundheads were to win, the country would fall into the hands of zealots. He felt there was no choice.

MEG: T'was a good man, his lordship. A kind man.

ANNE: If we had but world enough and time... Had I but known how precious was our time together.

MEG: Aye.

ANNE: Meg, have you had word of your son?

MEG: No, but I pray for him.

ANNE: I am so sorry.

Silence.

ANNE: I want you to know, I'd never abandon you and Bess. *Pause.* We are a small parish. The church cannot afford to feed everyone. And if the time comes when Cromwell's men march on Little Brideford, we cannot leave these people alone and vulnerable. I've decided to shelter the women from the village. And I hope to offer my protection to Joan Rainsford, the cunning woman.

MEG: She ain't a Christian.

A silence.

ANNE: Joan is my half-sister. She is my father's child with a maidservant who once worked in the house.

MEG: Aye. Katherine Rainsford. T'was John Rainsford's daughter. I remember.

ANNE: You knew?

MEG: Everyone knew.

ANNE: She is now my only living family. I'm bound to help her if I can. We must be generous with what little we've got. Joan is a poor, lonely woman with nowhere to go. And I believe she's ailing.

MEG: Folk reckon she's a witch. Holds a Black Mass in the woods.

ANNE: I don't care what comes from the mouths of others. We cannot allow ourselves to be overcome by the suspicions of weak, stupid people.

MEG: You're too young to remember when they tried five women in the village for witchcraft and hanged them. Years ago now.

ANNE: Five women?

MEG: Upon my honour. Mary Goodman. Lizzy Cradock. Avis Guthrie. Verity Burgess. Grace Keene—she were my cousin. Tried, found guilty and hanged, they were. In the town square.

ANNE: All five?

MEG: There'd been a bad harvest that year and a disease wot took away half the cattle in the parish. And three newborn babes, all die in the same week. Signs, they said. Got the first to confess—on the rack. Lizzy, it were. And she names the others.

ANNE: How wicked people are...

MEG: You know what folk are like, ma'am...gotta have someone to blame for their misfortunes.

ANNE: What proof did they have?

MEG: What proof did they need?

ANNE: But that is madness...it is condemnable!

MEG: I were a young lass but I'll not forget it 'til the day I die. Weren't no one to lift a finger to help those poor wretches. Their own families, friends, neighbours. Good, god-fearing people. Folk were afeared they'd be next for the noose. All afeared of each other. *Pause.* People know Mad Joan ain't a woman of God. If we take her in... And if the Puritans come... God forbid *we* should be suspected of practicing witchcraft.

ANNE: And what of poor Joan? What of Christian charity?

MEG: We got to look out for ourselves, m'lady.

7

1936. London.

PAMELA: The next day when I was in the office, David Stern sidled up to me and asked me what I thought about Dawson's pro-Germany policy. I told him I didn't really do politics and began to walk faster down the corridor. Stern has very short legs and had to trot next to me to keep up, but still he persisted. Mrs. More... you and I write for a newspaper with the largest circulation in the nation. You must have an opinion on Hitler. I walked a bit faster and Stern began to perspire. Hitler, Hitler, Hitler. Was this all anyone wanted to talk about? Yes, of course I do, I replied. He...he has kept the Communists at bay. I stopped to face Stern, feeling rather proud of myself. To tell the truth, I don't think I would especially like to have Hitler running *my* country, but when faced with such opposition I tend to become quarrelsome. (Ask Francis—he knows all too well.) Stern simply smiled and then looked sad. Yes, he has overthrown the Communists, but that's because everyone's been imprisoned or killed. My dear Mrs. More, the German Chancellor is eliminating the people he considers 'undesirables'. People who are not of his religious persuasion or ethnic background, people who have physical and mental illnesses. 'Degenerates', unfit to breed.

I wasn't sure where this was going but Stern looked so earnest, mopping his furrowed, clammy brow with his rumpled handkerchief. For a moment I thought, I wonder if Stern is married. He does always look so dishevelled, poor dear. The handkerchief looked as if it had been used many times before and there was a stain on his tie. The Nazis are pursuing a policy that is designed to exclude anyone who is not of the Aryan race, anyone not supporting the Nazi Party. Mrs. More, do you understand what is happening in Germany? German Jews—German citizens—are being stripped of their rights. They are not allowed to hold certain jobs or live in certain areas. Their shops are being closed down. Their children are being turned out of schools. How do you know all this? I asked, feeling overwhelmed. I have cousins who live in Berlin, Mrs. More, he replied. I was at a loss. I don't really know any Jews, I said. I suddenly realised that Stern himself was probably Jewish. Do you have children? He asked suddenly. No, I replied, confused. Well, Mrs. More, let's say you did...and let's say one of those children had been born with some mental or physical problems. And then the state offered to take your child away. For treatment, they said. But really, they were having the child sterilized. Or worse...euthanized.

I dropped my handbag and all my things fell out onto the floor. Stern stooped to help me collect them. He took my hand and patted it. Mrs. More—I know I am going on quite a bit. No, Mr. Stern, I whispered, it's quite alright. I wanted to have a word with you about your feature with Wallis Simpson, he continued. She's a very influential woman, Mrs. More. Some say the King is quite serious about her, that he wants to marry her. And if it comes to the Simpson woman or the crown...it isn't certain what he will choose. (How was it that it seemed as if everyone knew about the King's infatuation with the charwoman and I didn't?) Please consider your position. Our very own king is much in favour of the Nazi Party, which would be a terrible thing for Britain. Imagine this...what if you were shut out by society...you were fired from your job because of your political or religious beliefs. What if there were certain neighbourhoods from which you were barred? I paused. I suppose I would go out to the West Country. Where the family home is, I added feebly. And what if...? He started. What if...? I echoed him. Mrs. More, what if there was a war? What if Britain was under attack? And then we both fell silent, realizing that neither of us had an answer.

8

2014. London. Celia is with Tamara, a stylist and branding consultant. Lucy enters with dry-cleaning.

CELIA: Lucy, did you pick up the groceries on your way home from dropping off Georgina at swimming? We're completely out of milk.

LUCY: Sorry. I forgot. I'll go back out again later and get them. I remembered to get your dry-cleaning though.

CELIA: Thank you, Lucy. You've been fantastic.

LUCY: Jeremy wanted me to remind you his mother's birthday is this weekend.

CELIA: I suppose he wants me to get her a present, does he? Don't know why he can't ask me himself...

LUCY: And Georgina has a doctor's appointment tomorrow after school.

CELIA: Oh god, I have meetings all day. Could you take her?

LUCY: I have to go to my meeting then.

CELIA: A meeting for...? Oh, right. Well, it won't matter if you miss one, will it? I don't know what we'd do without you. Sorry, this is Tamara. She's a stylist. She's helping me 're-brand' my look. Lucy's an old friend of mine from unie who's staying with me for a while.

TAMARA: How sweet. Are you travelling?

LUCY: No, I live in London. I'm just unemployed.

CELIA: She's also helping taking care of my daughter while we find a new nanny.

TAMARA: Nightmare. Anyway...

Celia takes notes while Tamara talks.

TAMARA: People see you as a package—the high-flying career, the book, the woman. Especially now that you're in the public eye so much, giving talks, giving interviews. You're...what....34? You dress like you're in your 50s. You're trying to be taken seriously by looking mumsy. And I'm going to give you the number of a very good personal trainer. She does *everyone*. Helen Mirren, Rachel Weiss. *Whispers*. The Duchess of Cambridge. She's totally booked most of the time so don't be surprised if you have to take a 5am slot.

CELIA: 5am?

TAMARA: And I'm going to send you to a nutritionist.

Tamara peers at Celia's face.

TAMARA: Have you had anything done?

CELIA: No.

TAMARA: And you're...34...

CELIA: Do I look older?

TAMARA: I always think, if you start maintaining earlier rather than later, it means less work when you're *really* old. What we want to do is go for younger, sexier. Grow your hair out. Maybe soften your face with some highlights. Make you look more feminine. I'm seeing heels. Like real heels—not that kitten heel rubbish. Skirts. Soft, sheer blouses.

CELIA: To be honest, I've gained a bit of weight over the past few years...stress, you know... Oh god.

TAMARA: What?

CELIA: I was just thinking about those 5am personal training sessions.

TAMARA: You'll love them. Although I should warn you...some people vomit during their first session with Andrea. I mean, if you're not used to being pushed like that. Ok, this is what we're going to do. We're going to go for a kind of luxurious intelligence with a whiff of yummy-mummy. The thing is, right, that you're obviously a very capable, intelligent, career-minded woman. But we need to soften that. To remind people you're an attractive, sexual being. I know it's going to be a lot of effort but I think you'll find it will be worth it. I promise. You've probably worked quite hard to get where you are now, so you owe it to yourself to do this. Especially now when you have the book and these media appearances. And of course, if you're thinking about going to politics—

CELIA: Well, it was just a thought. That's awfully far away.

TAMARA: But this will make a good foundation for your public image. You need to build up your social capital. Never hurts to plan.

Celia takes notes.

CELIA: Right... Highlights. Nutritionist. Sheer blouses. *Pause.* I've just had an idea! Tamara, do you have an extra few minutes? Do you think you could take a look at Lucy?

TAMARA: I do have an appointment with this MP in a couple hours...

LUCY: Oh...really...I'm all right, thanks.

CELIA: It will be fun, Lucy. Just another few minutes? Lucy's trying to find a job and I think she could do with a little refresher.

LUCY: Really, you don't need to—

CELIA: She hasn't been very successful in job interviews I think it will make a world of difference. Of course she's gorgeous already, but it might give her a confidence boost.

Tamara appraises Lucy.

TAMARA: For starters, your hair is looking a bit limp. I would take at least four or five inches off so it looks healthy again. And go lighter. Highlights. Definitely. Do you always wear trainers?

CELIA: She has a very casual look.

TAMARA: I hate casual. Casual says frumpy. Casual says you don't care. With a body like yours, I would stay away from such a soft silhouette. It isn't very flattering. I would go for structured, clean lines.

CELIA: That's what I was thinking.

TAMARA: Pencil skirts. That sort of thing. And define your eyes. Give yourself a little colour. Are you wearing any makeup at all? You're not, are you? And you might want to look at your diet. Your skin looks awfully sallow. Do you work out?

LUCY: Not really.

TAMARA: I thought not. I would put you on the same regime as Celia. And see a nutritionist. You're probably eating too much wheat. It gives that bloated look, you know? I never touch the stuff. It's poison. No wheat. No dairy. No sugar.

LUCY: I'm not really...

TAMARA: You're not really what?

LUCY: I'm not really into this sort of thing.

TAMARA: This sort of thing?

LUCY: I don't really care what people think of me, of what I'm wearing, or if I'm fat.

TAMARA: No? Not at all?

LUCY: I don't think it's important.

TAMARA: You mean you would show up to a job interview wearing, for instance, that?

LUCY: Of course not.

TAMARA: But I thought you said you don't care what people think of you, of what you're wearing.

LUCY: I don't.

TAMARA: I see. Well, some advice. Gratis. You're a package. Celia is a package. And if you want to get anywhere in the world, I think...and really, it's just my humble opinion as someone who's worked in fashion, marketing and PR, you are the image you project. You are a brand. This is how the world works. I understand this. Celia understands this. You may not like it, but most people understand this. *Pause.* And I wouldn't say fat per se. Overdoing it a bit, don't you think?

Tamara gathers her things and prepares to leave.

TAMARA: I must dash, but do remind me to give you the name of that personal shopper I mentioned at Harvey Nicks, Celia.

CELIA: Thanks, Tamara.

TAMARA: Ciao, darling!

Tamara does air kisses and exits.

CELIA: I can't believe I've been walking around looking the way I do for so long.

LUCY: What's wrong with the way you look?

CELIA: I'm turning into a hideous old woman. Shocking.

LUCY: No, you're not. You're letting her brainwash you. Are you really going to go to personal training sessions at five o'clock in the morning?

CELIA: Lucy, I'm in the middle of a book tour, and a I have a number of very public media engagements. Did I tell you I'm going to be on telly? Do you know how many pounds the camera adds?

LUCY: But you look fine.

CELIA: I was stuck in traffic the other day. I sat there for a while and looked at myself in the rear-view mirror. I wondered how I'd suddenly become so old. One minute I'm a leggy eighteen year-old going off to Durham and the next I'm a haggard-looking woman in a rumpled suit with a child. Driving a people carrier. Jeremy married a size six and a pretty face. I don't know if I'd fancy me anymore either.

LUCY: Celia...

CELIA: It was working. It wasn't perfect but it was working. We...made sense together. It's not realistic to expect wild passion after eight years, is it?

LUCY: You're being too hard on yourself.

CELIA: Am I?

LUCY: You're doing your best.

CELIA: We haven't...you know...in a long time. We did try, for a while. Dressing up, role-play, you know... It's just that...more than a month...three months... I know that things shift as you get older. That you can't always expect the same kind of intimacy after a while. *Pause.* Gosh—it's so late already. And Nick's—that place with the lovely organic veg—closes soon. Do you think you could just pop out now and do the shopping? I would, but I have about a million things to do.

9

1646. Brookfield House. Anne is on her knees, trying to pray, in the chapel on the estate.

ANNE: Oh Lord, I know I'm so seldom in your house and I haven't proven my faith in many months. I am probably the last person you'd expect to ask for your help, but I am struggling, Lord, and I need your guidance. If you can hear me, give me a sign. I have been doing what I think is true to help these people but I cannot do it alone. Show me in some way that I'm not leading them to their deaths. Help me find the resolve, the grace and the strength to persevere.

Anne tries to pray again in silence.

Lord, why have you abandoned me?

Anne opens her locket with a miniature of William inside.

You have abandoned me too, William. You've left me on my own. What a sad and joyless winter it has been. They say that in London the Puritans have forbidden Christmas. The harvest was poor and the soldiers left us with nothing. You are a good Royalist woman. His Majesty will be most grateful. William, we will soon be going hungry and I know not what to do. I long for the days before all this. I long for you. Nothing is as it was. There's scarcely a man or boy in the parish who hasn't fallen in battle, leaving their families to beg by the roadside. And hardly any able-bodied men left to take up arms, to protect the village. His Majesty has not been seen for some time and his armies are weak. I worry we are on the verge of defeat. And I fear for what may happen to all of us.

Anne gets up and looks at her hands.

These last four years have aged me. The lines in my skin have deepened and my hands are ruddy and coarse. If anyone met me, they would not think I was a gentlewoman, but a common labourer. My love, you would scarcely recognize me yourself. *Pause*. I have not a soul to turn to in my darkest hour. You have been gone these two years and left me no children for company. But perhaps it was God's will that all my babies should be stillborn and I should be barren. *Pause*. Yesterday evening I walked down to the river behind the potato field and stood on the bank while the sun set. For a moment, my love, I thought of filling my pockets with stones and walking into the cold water. But I was too afraid. What if I were to die and was not in a state of grace? They say Hell is the preserve of the wicked and faithless. But what if there is simply... *Pause*. Nothing? An endless nothing. What if there is nothing, no one, to await me on the other side of the river?

10

1936. London.

PAMELA: When I first met the King, or Wales as everyone called him when he was still the Prince, at first I didn't realize who he was. I was at the Coconut Club a few years back—Francis had just gone to the bar and I had a cigarette but no light. And with the holder clenched between my teeth I was about to turn to Jack Harris when this somewhat petite gentleman lit my cigarette. Allow me, he drawled. Thank you, I drawled in reply. I turned to Flossie Brackenberry, who was smiling beatifically. She curtsied. I took a look at the gentleman again and lo and behold, it was the Prince. I quickly followed suit. Lady Pamela More, Sir, I said. He smiled and said, yes...charming...charming... And then walked off. Just like that. You could have knocked me over with a feather. I thought to myself he'd make a decent king. A refreshing change from his father with his bushy beard and deep-set eyes. Less Zeus and more Apollo.

I had not, however, met the celebrated Mrs. Simpson. So when I arrived, notebook in hand, for our appointed rendezvous, I was quite unprepared to meet a rather severe American with a face like a charwoman. They say the she's quite a clothes horse but I personally would say she is more horse than clothes. Very hard features. My mother would describe her as a 'handsome' woman, meaning someone who isn't altogether unattractive but looks more like a man than is entirely appropriate. During her gown fitting, Wallis explained, you see now that his majesty and I are such close *friends*, he insists that I accompany him everywhere. I was surprised at her brazen statement and assumed that she was exaggerating, as most vulgar Americans do. One cannot possibly be seen in the same gown twice. And we ladies of Baltimore know how to dress. (Where indeed was Baltimore? I wondered.) Wallis chattered on about her impending divorce from her husband and her relationship with the King. I think she was trying desperately to impress me—she kept going on about how inseparable they were and how 'the boss' (as she *so* inappropriately referred to His Majesty) simply couldn't do without her.

Near the end of our têt-a-têt, I thought I saw a man, hiding in the bushes, watching us through the window. And then fifteen minutes later, I saw him again. A chap in a bowler hat and a trench coat was clearly watching us through binoculars. I assumed it must have been some awful little gossip-monger from The Daily Mail trying to listen in and spy on me. We'll just see about that, I said to myself. I slyly wended my way to the side of the building and caught the little snoop in the bushes. Whack! I whacked him over the head with my umbrella. Take that, you vile man! I shouted. Whack. How dare you try to steal my story like that? Whack whack. He cowered and covered his face with his arms. Go back to The Daily Mail and tell your editors never dare to tread on the toes of The Times ever again! I cried as I gave him a good sound thrashing with my umbrella. Madam! Desist! I am not a journalist! He protested. Well, who in god's name are you, then? Whack whack. Mrs. More, stop hitting me with your umbrella! I froze. How do you know my name? I demanded, holding my weapon aloft. To cut a long story short, the man—whose name was Charlie and was rather handsome—claimed he worked for some secret branch of the government and had been assigned to watch over the Simpson woman. After our initial to-do with the umbrella I began interrogating him, and when Charlie realized I was going to make a fuss he grudgingly agreed to take me for a coffee in a dingy little café nearby.

Charlie leaned in closely, gesturing for me to do the same. I felt as if I were in a film. There are certain parties who believe Wales is not fit to be King...that he is too sympathetic to the Germans. Now that Hitler's marched into the Rhineland, some people believe it may come to blows. I thought the League of Nations settled these kinds of things, I retorted. Charlie grabbed my hand across the table. I was electrified by his soft touch. The faint smell of stale coffee and burnt toast mingled with the sweetness of his cologne. The Prime Minister himself has an interest in the affair between Wallis Simpson and the King. Affair? I puzzled. That woman went on and on about how close she is with His Majesty but I assumed she was just being obnoxious. Charlie lit another cigarette, inhaling deeply. Mrs. More, Wallis Simpson is the consort of the King. She is his lover. I froze. I felt the blood drain from my face. His *what*? I said softly. They are quite inseparable and the King has made it known he intends to marry this woman once her divorce has been finalized. Marry? Marry? That charwoman...the King of England was in love with *her*? It couldn't be possible.

Well, something has to be done to pry His Majesty from her greedy tendrils? Actually, Charlie replied, we are trying to encourage her relationship with His Majesty in any way possible. The man is unfit to be king and could possibly endanger the future of this country. If it's a choice between the throne and his lady-love, the Prime Minister and quite a few other people sincerely hope he will choose her and leave his brother the Duke of York to reign. Mrs. More... Our sovereign is an easily-influenced dimwit interested only in his tailor, golf and sunbathing on the Mediterranean. And if he's idiotic enough to fall for the charms of such a person as Mrs. Earnest Simpson of Baltimore, USA, then what else might he fall prey to?

My husband is in the House of Lords. I couldn't possibly involve myself in a plot to de-throne the king. Francis would be so upset with me. But then I had a thought: Charlotte would be ever so jealous, were she to find out. My sister thinks she's the only one in the family who's ever done anything exciting. She's so snide...hello from Rio de Janeiro...hello from Ceylon! She's not going to be the only one doing something interesting. And besides, Charlie was really rather good-looking and quite difficult to resist when he smiled. I told Charlie that of course he was going to need my help.

11

1646. Brookfield House. Meg sings the English folk song 'Barbara Allen' loudly and off-key, hacking away at the soil like a madwoman.

MEG: In Scarlet Town where I was born, there lived a fair maid dwellin'. Made many a youth cry well a day, her name was Barbara Allen. It was in the merry month of May when green buds they were swellin'. Sweet William came from the West Country and he courted Barbara Allen.

Bess enters and watches Meg for a moment.

MEG: In Scarlet Town where I was born, there lived a fair maid dwellin'—

BESS: Ye've already sung that verse.

MEG: It's the only one I knows.

BESS: But everyone knows Barb'ry Allen.

MEG: In Scarlet town where I was born, there lived a fair maid dwellin'—

BESS: Ye want to sing summat else then, eh?

Meg hacks away at the ground, continuing to sing.

BESS: Ye want to rest a spell?

MEG: In Scarlet Town where I was born—

BESS: What's got into ye?

Meg pauses in her tilling and is silent for a moment.

MEG: Bess, we're livin' at the mercy 'a these folk. We work their land 'n we're bound to 'em like slaves.

BESS: Meg, don't talk like tha'.

MEG: When the King called for an army, Lord William took the men 'n boys from 'round here, the ones that worked on the farm, servants, tenants on the land, men from the village. Me man said it was our duty to the King, our duty to Sir William. His lordship didn't know nowt about fightin'. None of 'em knew hardly anythin' about fightin' proper soldiers. Me man never held a gun in his life. Me husband, me boys. All gone. Lost everything. Then the soldiers took our crops 'n our livestock. Fer the King, says they. A good Royalist household gives all it can to the army. So we gave all.

BESS: Lady Anne said it were our duty.

MEG: Duty! *Meg spits.* Duty to who?

BESS: Our duty to the king, Meg!

MEG: No one feels a duty to us common folk. What cared our king for us? Folk says Oliver Cromwell's but a Cambridgeshire farmer. And a pious man. Says his army prays afore battles.

BESS: Meg, what are you saying?

MEG: What if the King weren't chosen by god to rule? What if it's god's will that Cromwell and Fairfax should win? Plain Christian men. Not kings.

BESS: Meg!

MEG: What if we had a vote, eh? What if we could vote on who gets to be king? On who gets to tell us what to do and who owns the land? What if we had our own land? Our own lives to do as we please with them? *Laughs.* Lass, I'm weary of bowin' and scrapin'.

BESS: Meg, you can't say that!

MEG: And why not?

BESS: That's treason. *Pause.* Ain't it?

MEG: It treasonous to want yer freedom?

BESS: Well, then it ain't loyal to her ladyship.

MEG: If my Tom hadn't been 'loyal'...if my boys hadn't been 'loyal'...maybe they'd still be alive. Maybe I'd still have my own roof over my head with my own hearth and my own garden to till. My own family...

BESS: Lady Anne is a good woman, a kind woman. She cares for us. More 'n anyone else in Little Brideford.

MEG: But she ain't one of us, Bess! Think she'd be out pickin' potatoes and milkin' cows if this war hadn't come?

BESS: But the war did come. She took you in.

MEG: Never wanted her charity anyhow...

BESS: She ain't like folk in the village. They'd leave us to die by the roadside 'fore they took us in. Her ladyship's just tryin' to be a good Christian by givin' shelter to a poor, friendless woman.

Joan appears, unseen.

MEG: She's a witch. We'll all be damned if we shelter her.

BESS: She ain't a witch!

MEG: Don't matter what she is or what she ain't. People *reckon* she's a witch. All that matters.

BESS: She's an innocent woman, Meg. She's just a healer. And besides, what good are prayers and faith without Christian deeds? We can't let her starve.

MEG: What about us starvin'?

BESS: What about charity?

MEG: Ain't no charity left in the world.

BESS: Mad Joan helped me mam when me sister were a wee lass. Had a fever that wouldn't break. Mam feared it were the plague, but Mad Joan saved her life. Gave her summat and the fever broke the next mornin'. Me mam wouldn't say nowt against her. Ain't her fault she's peculiar. Reckon she went a bit mad when they put the Scold's Bridle on her all them years back. I can still see it. That metal cage over her head, holdin' her tongue down, ripping her mouth apart. Locked in the stocks for two days with no food nor water.

MEG: Showin' other womenfolk what happens to scolds 'n witches.

BESS: We have to protect her, Meg. It might be the noose next time.

MEG: It might be the noose for all of us! What if we were accused of witchcraft, Bess? Ain't been too long since they hanged all those women in Norfolk.

BESS: Think they'd do that to us? For shelterin' Joan?

MEG: They'll say we was all witches.

Silence.

MEG: Tom wanted to take the boys and go to Virginia. Make a new start. Said in the colonies in the New World we could have our own land. I was too afraid to go. Maybe I shoulda said yes. (*Meg looks around and lowers her voice.*) Now Bess...can ye keep a secret?

BESS: Aye.

MEG: You mustn't tell anyone.

BESS: Aye.

MEG: My boy, Michael... He ain't missing.

BESS: What do you mean?

MEG: He weren't killed neither. He went over to Cromwell.

BESS: Cromwell!

MEG: Hush, now, ye foolish girl! Ye can't tell a soul.

BESS: You said he were dead, Meg.

MEG: Couldn't tell no one, could I?

BESS: But—

MEG: If Cromwell 'n Fairfax's armies come to Little Brideford, my Michael'll be with them.

BESS: What will you do?

MEG: I'll join him.

BESS: Meg! You can't join Cromwell! He betrayed the king!

MEG: Bugger the king. What's he ever done for us, besides get us into this war?

BESS: That's treason.

MEG: Ain't no such thing no more. King's armies are losing. Think everyone knows it too.

BESS: How can you say that?

MEG: You should join us, pet.

BESS: I can't leave her ladyship. Don't know how you can neither.

MEG: Michael's my boy. My blood. He's all I have left on this earth.

BESS: I can't. What will happen to her ladyship? What will happen to Mad Joan?

MEG: It's god's will, whatever happens to any of us.

Meg sees Joan.

MEG: How long you been standin' there?

JOAN: Long enough.

MEG: You going to tell her ladyship?

JOAN: You going to tell folk in the village I'm a witch?

MEG: No.

JOAN: Then I s'pose I'll hold my tongue.

Silence.

MEG: And ye can't tell her ladyship 'bout this. It's our secret, Bess. Understand?

BESS: But...

MEG: Swear it, Bess.

BESS: I swear.

12

1936. London.

PAMELA: Tonight, I found myself at a party at the German Embassy. Charlie said Wales and the Simpson Woman would be there. I was to pay particular attention to the goings-on between the charwoman and von Ribbentrop, the German ambassador. Charlie said Wallis was so close to the King that she was privy to state secrets, and it would be a disaster if she was passing information to the Germans. If I was to see her alone with von Ribbentrop, I was to tell him straightaway. So there I was, at this rather strange social gathering, on the pretense of representing The Times, but actually spying on the King of England, the German Ambassador and the charwoman. We heard a well-fed Brunhilde sing Wagner, and there were lots of toasts to the health of the Reich and the alliance between Britain and Germany. Charlie had shuffled off somewhere, and hardly anyone spoke a word to me. I realized I was completely on my own and felt the cold panic rising in my throat. Pamela More, I said to myself, you are in over your head. You're just a woman with a column and a nose for fashion. What are you playing at? But then I thought about what Stern said about Hitler shoving the Jews off the pier and all that. I started to wonder if it was true, about the children. But it was too awful to bear and I put it out of my mind at once.

What I've gathered is that Ambassador von Ribbentrop really is rather unsound. After striking up a conversation with an anxious little man working as some kind of undersecretary in the embassy, I learned his employer is erratic and shouts quite a lot. Doesn't keep appointments. Goes around upsetting the ambassadors to other countries. Apparently wants the entire embassy remodeled to suit his tastes and to fly the Nazi flag out the front. Well, if his tastes are anything like Mr. Hitler's, I can envision lots of black leather and enormous eagles all over the place. For a brief moment, I met the Ambassador who clicked his heels together in an alarming fashion as he shook my hand. I had barely been introduced when von Ribbentrop suddenly turned around, screamed in German at the undersecretary and marched away imperiously. It was utterly bizarre and *unspeakably* rude. I was just about to retreat to the bar to recover myself and gather my thoughts when I saw a woman appear, as if from nowhere, partway down the corridor. She lurked in the shadows, waiting for von Ribbentrop, and caught his arm as he passed her. I gasped. It was the charwoman! I tried to get as near as I could to the pair of them, slinking quietly closer, gripping my handbag nervously. I couldn't hear a thing but I watched as he stroked her cheek and she whispered something in his ear. They suddenly looked around and I hid. They parted ways, the ambassador going one way and the charwoman going the other.

I allowed Wallis to pass me and then followed her, wondering what she was up to next. She was heading towards the power room, so I fell back a few paces, allowed her to enter alone, waited a moment or two and walked in behind her. She stood at the mirror, refreshing her lipstick. Oh, hello, Pamela, she said. I wasn't aware you frequented the German Embassy. I'm here on an assignment from the paper, I coolly replied. His Majesty is on very close terms with the German Ambassador, Wallis explained, and of course he simply cannot go anywhere without me. I took a gamble. Are you on as close terms with Herr von Ribbentrop as his majesty is, then? Joacim is such a lot of fun and His Majesty insists we dine with him all the time. Between you and me, I think the ambassador has a little schoolboy crush on me. Oh, really? I pried. Well, yes, but my heart belongs to His Majesty. What people don't understand is that his family really is very cruel to him and couldn't give a damn if he was happy or not. It makes me so very, very sad. I know our little *arrangement* is a bit...*inconvenient* to some people, but of course I only want what's best for David. (David? She calls him David?) Earnest has been very understanding about the whole thing. I have told David I would fold my tent and steal away quietly if he asked me and sometimes I think... She trailed off, sniffing ever so slightly as if she might cry. Sometimes I think maybe it would be for the best if I disappeared. It would be less complicated, wouldn't it? You see, I have come to feel so very at home here in London. It is a bit odd, not being British, but not really feeling very American back at home, in Baltimore. You never really know who your real friends are. Or if you *have* any real friends. It's very easy to feel quite alone at times, especially when everyone who's ever laid eyes on you can drop you like yesterday's news. Even David. And if he were to...drop me...I'll have lost everything.

For a moment, I felt a little sorry for the charwoman. I felt the instinct to reach out to her. Take her hand or put an arm around those bony shoulders. But there was something I didn't entirely trust. They say Earnest Simpson lost quite a bit in the crash in '29 and keeps his wife on a tight leash, at least financially, if not morally. No bespoke ball gowns for the charwoman when she was simply Mrs. Simpson, lately of Baltimore, lately Mrs. Spenser. Not only has she been married twice and was most likely to be divorced twice, her maiden name was Bessie Wallis Warfield. (How hideous.) Until she met the Prince, she was always rather out of funds. 'I only want what's best for David'. My foot. I only want what's best for moi. Even if that includes the attentions of the King of England *and* the ambassador to the Third Reich. For all we knew, she was making secret night flights to Berlin and carrying on with Mr. Hitler himself, the traitor! All of a sudden there was a knock on the door and a voice said, Wallis...Wallis...my darling are you in there? You know your little kingy-wingy can't do his kingly duties without his wittle Wally-Wally... That two-timing, double-dealing American perked right up and called back, I'm coming my darling little kingy-wingy...now don't do anything naughty until I come out, do you hear? You be a good boy for Wally-Wally and she'll reward you. I nearly gagged. The filth. It was just too much.

I found Charlie as soon as I could and carted him off to the terrace. I recounted what I had gleaned from the evening in my spy-like fashion, all a-twitter. Charlie seemed very pleased, in his subdued manner. Well, not pleased as such, that the King's ill-advised consort was cavorting with Nazi officials and probably spilling the beans with every seductive whisper. But more than satisfied with what I had discovered. He said there were certain, influential people in the government who would value an eyewitness account of Wallis and von Ribbentrop's intimacy very highly. It was all quite thrilling. I didn't even mind the cross-looking Germans or the opera or von Ribbentrop marching around like an Alsatian. In the aftermath of it all, I had a bit too much champagne and Charlie had to take me home in his awfully nice motorcar. I felt rather daring as we sped along the dark London streets, with lovely Charlie at the wheel in his tailcoat.

13

2014. Celia's house. Celia is on her laptop. Lucy enters, startled.

CELIA: There you are.

LUCY: Hi.

CELIA: Did you take the car in to be looked at this morning?

LUCY: Yes.

CELIA: And you were home in time to let the painters in?

LUCY: Yes.

CELIA: I tried calling you to remind you but your phone was off.

LUCY: The battery died.

CELIA: It makes me nervous when I can't get a hold of you.

LUCY: Sorry, Celia. Wait, why are you home? I mean, why aren't you at work?

CELIA: Because Georgina has been suspended from school. They called me at work and dragged me down there to tell me she'd not only freed the class bunny from its cage but had been hitting the other children. Apparently this has been going on for some time. Why they didn't tell me sooner, I don't know. The headmistress claims that they haven't been able to get a hold of me. Did you know anything about this?

LUCY: No, but they don't really tell me anything. They just think I'm the hired help.

CELIA: This is a nightmare. What am I going to do with her now?

LUCY: I don't think you should worry too much. She's probably going through a phase.

CELIA: That may well be and I hope to god it's only a phase, but she's just been suspended from one of the best schools in London.

LUCY: I think you're overreacting.

CELIA: Overreacting?

LUCY: She hasn't been expelled.

CELIA: I don't want my daughter to have a permanent record.

LUCY: She's only seven.

CELIA: She needs to be able to get into good schools when she's older. I have her future to think about.

LUCY: I think you're worrying too much.

CELIA: You don't understand. This could be a real problem. What if she needs to see a psychiatrist?

LUCY: It might not be a bad idea.

CELIA: What do you mean?

LUCY: I love Georgina and she's pretty good with me, but...

CELIA: But?

LUCY: I've seen her be...a little aggressive with other children.

CELIA: Why didn't you say anything?

LUCY: Frankly, I thought you already knew.

CELIA: Well, I didn't know. And maybe if you had told me then she wouldn't have been suspended from school. I could have done something to prevent this. And the worst part is, I've missed a very important meeting at work. I mean, the school said it was practically an emergency so I left and went straight down there. Of course I asked if you could go instead but they said they couldn't release her to someone who wasn't her guardian. And I tried to call Jeremy but I'd forgotten that he's on another bloody business trip. Geneva. Or Frankfurt. I actually don't even remember. And it's not like he ever has to worry about this sort of thing. You can handle it, darling. You're better at that sort of thing than I am. I might as well be a single mother sometimes. With the book launch next week I've been so busy—

Celia's phone rings.

CELIA: Paul. Hi. Sorry I wasn't at the meeting today. I've been having a bit of a family-related crisis at home. *Pause.* No, no, it's nothing. Everyone's fine. Please tell Alexander that I'll catch up and he has nothing to worry about. Could you do me a favour? I need a copy of the minutes from you. I can go over it tonight and look at the contract as well. I just hate that I'm so behind now. *Pause.* I know it needs to be done before the markets open tomorrow morning. I said I would do it tonight. *Pause.* What do you mean—Michael gave it to you to finish? I've been in charge of the restructuring from the beginning, Paul. I know I haven't been in but I've been working from home. Well, I've been trying to work from home. *Pause.* I haven't fallen behind. *Pause.* I haven't been making mistakes. Fine. You're only doing this because this is going to be all over the FT soon and you want to make sure it's your name billed right up there with mine. So you can eventually take my job.

Celia hangs up.

CELIA: This is so frustrating! I can't even get any work done. I've been working on a major restructuring of the company and because I miss one stupid meeting, Paul's trying to take over the bloody thing.

LUCY: I'm sure it's not a big deal.

CELIA: Yes, it is. You never miss work. You must always be available, otherwise someone else will take the credit.

LUCY: They probably understand that it's important.

CELIA: Do they?

LUCY: She is your daughter.

CELIA: You can't miss meetings. You can't miss a phone call. You can't miss an opportunity to shine. If you've worked on a project you have to make sure your name is on it, that you get the credit for it.

LUCY: But they know you work hard. You work all the time, Celia.

CELIA: I can always work harder. And if I don't, there will be someone waiting to take my place, or worse, someone waiting to be promoted above me. *Pause.* Lucy, where were you earlier?

LUCY: Well...when Georgina's at school and you're at work, sometimes I go to the cafe down the road to work on job applications and write a bit.

CELIA: I see. Must be nice. To be able to do that. Go for a coffee in the middle of the afternoon. Turn your phone off. Have some time to yourself.

LUCY: I'm unemployed. It's what people do when they're unemployed.

CELIA: You know, I don't think I've ever been unemployed.

LUCY: Then you're lucky.

CELIA: I suppose I am.

LUCY: Celia...did you get a chance to read my manuscript?

CELIA: No. Sorry. I just haven't had any time.

14

1936. London.

PAMELA: So there we all were, at another one of Dawson's weekly meetings, but this time I could tell something was afoot. Dawson looked uneasy, perspiring ever so slightly beneath his little round spectacles as the rain trickled down the windows on the chilly December morning. Everyone watched him, waiting. Although this paper has always been an ardent supporter of his Majesty the King and would never do anything to compromise his reign, or be considered anything but patriotic and staunchly monarchist, he began…there has been a sea change in Fleet Street…and, it would seem, in Downing Street as well. I personally am disgusted by such mud-slinging and the feverish frenzies to which this growing scandal has given rise. But I am a newspaperman and The Times cannot refuse to provide breaking stories, otherwise our readers will seek them elsewhere. Cue tittering and whispering as Dawson looked out the window distractedly.

Apparently, the Fleet Street blackout regarding the King and the Simpson Woman had been broken. The Bishop of Bradford had made some speech questioning the King's 'need for divine guidance'. And suddenly every two-bit rag in the country decided that the gloves were off. Of course all the American papers had decided the gloves were off months ago and had been laughing up their sleeves at us for being so polite about the whole thing.

Dawson sighed. If it were up to me, The Times would not participate in such low gossip-mongering but we must sell papers. If it were up to me, he repeated (intimating heavily that it very much should be up to him), The Times would do nothing to jeopardize His Majesty's reign, which the stories of Mrs. Simpson's divorce will most assuredly do. The rumors that the King will leave the throne if he isn't allowed to marry Mrs. Simpson are growing stronger by the day. We can only hope that we do not have a revolution on our hands. People may protest if he steps down, and they may protest if he does not step down. A revolution, I thought. Men in the street with guns. Francis driving a bus. Charlie coming to my rescue and fighting off the Nazis with his bare hands. Or maybe me coming to Charlie's rescue, wearing a babushka. I was getting carried away. Dawson was still speaking, something about the integrity of the press and the sanctity of the monarchy and what a loss it would be if His Majesty abdicated.

I had become rather cross. Before I knew what I was doing, I interrupted him. What a loss it would be? I echoed, indignantly. I said I felt it was absurd that we had to lie to protect that dreadful woman and that silly little man. Dawson then became quite cross himself. Just because you wrote one piece on Mrs. Simpson's wardrobe doesn't mean you have any kind of political understanding. Why don't you go back to hats and gowns, Pamela? Everyone was silent. Have you ever met him? I demanded. I have. He's a careless, selfish, silly little man who's going to get us all into trouble with that other silly little man in Germany. And I know you think Hitler is just a splendid chap, but Hitler is killing people. He's killing *children*. I know no one wants another war, but where is this all leading? Who's in charge in this country anyway? We might have another war whether we like it or not. We might have another war when we find Hitler on our doorstep, after leading our nice, quiet, blinkered lives. And then where will we be? Dawson was purple in the face, temporarily unable to speak. David Stern smiled at me from across the table. There was a good deal of commotion and whispering as I put on my hat and coat and tried to make an exit as gracefully as possible.

When I left The Times, I did something I have never done before in my life. I went to a pub. Alone. And had a few very stiff drinks. Francis was in Scotland playing golf and I couldn't bear to return to an empty house with the anticipation of getting the sack hanging over my head. Tottering home a couple hours later, I suddenly had the sensation that I was being followed. As I approached my front steps, I nearly screamed as I felt a hand on my arm. But it was only Charlie, thank heavens. Darling, lovely Charlie. What a sight for sore eyes, I said to him, as I struggled to unlock the door. He said he wanted to pass on a message of thanks from those above him. My information about the Simpson Woman being in league with von Ribbentrop had helped tip the scales in favor of the government rejecting any proposal from the King to marry her. And those on the inside were already fairly certain that Wales would indeed abdicate, leaving his brother the Duke of York to reign. A stable family man with no apparent penchant for yachting, American divorcées or Fascists.

There was something in the air that evening—perhaps a sense of victory—though I would like to remind you that I was *quite* tight at this point. I wandered around the place, letting my cape hang off one shoulder and taking my hair down. I ordered Charlie to pour us a brandy and I sashayed over to the gramophone to peruse the record collection. I put on the first record I saw, which just happened by *pure chance* to be Bizet's Carmen. It felt like we were the only people in the world, protecting the Empire against forces of evil. I thought about the terrible Simpson woman and the terrible Mr. von Ribbentrop. The terrible Mr. Hitler and what David Stern said about the terrible things he was doing to those children. How terrible it all was. Take me! I cried. Take me now, whilst you can! Charlie looked at me in surprise. Take me, you great brute! You Tartar! Ravage me! Ravage you? He replied, confused. I think the word you're looking for is ravish, Pamela. I said ravage and I meant ravage! I was aflame. What on earth are you waiting for? Throw me down upon the bed and maul me! Carmen played in the background, driving me on. He was the matador and I the bull. Or vice-versa. He the bull and I the matador. Or—no, it does work better the other way round. Charlie with his red cape, fanning the flames of desire. I was the bull *and* the matador *and* Carmen all at once. I was overcome. And I was drunk. Pamela, he said, you are drunk. Charlie, I said, don't be such a bore. My matador, my Tartar! I am not a Tartar, he protested. I removed my cape, swinging it off my shoulders with a flourish. Olé! I cried. I could see Charlie was sweating. My magic was working. Olé! I insisted, waving the cape at him. Charlie sat on the bed, loosening his collar nervously. I began to unbutton my dress. Oh dear, said Charlie. I am a woman who gets what she wants, and indeed, I did.

Francis is as solid as a rock. We're very fond of each other, of course. We were rather long in the tooth when we became engaged. Charlotte and Peter had already been married for quite some time at that point, which was embarrassing, as I came out several seasons before her. (Charlotte always was a bit fast.) I sometimes wonder if I'm too much for Francis, but I didn't want to be left on the shelf. Mother used to tell me, if you're not careful you'll end up like Aunt Constance. The suffragette. Used to chain herself to the railings, go on marches, get arrested—that sort of thing. Embarrassed the family terribly. Mother was very firm Charlotte and I were not to take Aunt Constance for a role model, that we were to marry and lead respectable lives.

When I woke up next to Charlie the next morning, I didn't feel half as sorry as I should have. I'd never done anything like that before, but how often does one get the opportunity? Of course a divorce would kill Daddy. It simply isn't done in our family. Then I would end up like the King's charwoman…divorced and having an affair with a strange man. He does have rather beautiful blue eyes and such soft, downy hair. Charlie that is. Not his majesty.

15

2014. London. Celia comes home from work. Lucy is doing something domestic, like folding laundry.

LUCY: I saw you on ITV this morning.

CELIA: How do you think it went? I had to be in the studio so bloody early for makeup. I must have had the worst circles under my eyes.

LUCY: I thought you looked great. I think it went really well.

CELIA: Thank you. You're so sweet. By the way, I have some really good news for you. I've convinced my publisher to speak to one of the other editors, someone in fiction, to read your book.

LUCY: Really?

CELIA: I mean, I can't guarantee anything but I think getting your foot in the door is the important part.

LUCY: So you read it?

CELIA: Well, most of it anyway. I never have time to read.

LUCY: What did you think?

CELIA: It was very…dark. Not really my kind of book…you know me, I'm more into mysteries. I like books that distract me from my life. But, I have to admit. It was very good.

LUCY: Thank you.

CELIA: Very distressing, I thought. But I know some people like that kind of thing. Have you met with anyone about this before? Agents? Publishers? Editors?

LUCY: No.

CELIA: Let me give you a little advice. Personally, I wouldn't say anything about your own...issues.

LUCY: My own issues?

CELIA: Oh, you know, the drinking and the antidepressants and...well, we both know you don't have the cleanest track record with drugs...

LUCY: But I wrote a book about addiction.

CELIA: It's not like it's an autobiography.

LUCY: No, but it's been informed by my own experiences.

CELIA: You don't have to tell them *everything*.

LUCY: Celia, I really appreciate you doing this for me—I really do—but I'm not going to lie about who I am.

CELIA: No one's asking you to lie. You just don't want to come across as unprofessional.

LUCY: Do you think I'm unprofessional?

CELIA: I think you know what I'm getting at.

LUCY: No, I don't.

CELIA: Sometimes, you can be a little…

LUCY: A little what?

CELIA: I just want to make sure that you take full advantage of this opportunity.

LUCY: You sound like you don't trust me.

CELIA: No, it's not that, it's just… Did you read my book?

Silence.

LUCY: I did, actually.

CELIA: I know I'm no Tolstoy, but I thought it might help you.

LUCY: Why would it help me? I'm not trying to climb the corporate ladder.

CELIA: I don't think you understood it.

LUCY: Celia, let's be honest. You didn't write it for women like me.

CELIA: I wrote it for all women.

LUCY: But it's really only for highly educated women working for big corporations.

CELIA: Maybe I use a very specific demographic as an example, but—

LUCY: It wasn't written for women like me, for teachers or writers or, I don't know, someone who works in Tesco. People who don't make much money.

CELIA: I'm trying to give women practical advice, which, I should add, a lot of people seem to really appreciate.

LUCY: But what you're saying is that if they don't work all the time, if they're not perfect, they're failures.

CELIA: Hard work is important.

LUCY: What if you work hard and you still can't make enough money to live on?

CELIA: I'm not saying that—

LUCY: Whatever happened to holding the system accountable?

CELIA: That's awfully vague. What do you mean by the system?

LUCY: Corporations. Corporate structures—hiring practices. The government—employment policies. Society, for god's sake. You can't always blame individual women for their own failings.

CELIA: There's no need to constantly beat the drum of feminism. Look, I've worked bloody hard to get where I am now and I did it on my own.

LUCY: You didn't do it on your own. You had parents who supported you. You had money to go to school and you had connections to get good, well-paying jobs. You could afford childcare to work long hours. Not everyone has that kind of support. We don't start on some big, level playing field.

CELIA: Yes, so I was fortunate. But it wasn't all luck. It was hard work. I've always worked fucking hard, Lucy. Everyone needs to make the most of what they're given.

LUCY: You say that if everyone just works hard, they'll succeed. Even when you know it isn't true. I worked hard. I worked myself into the ground. Until I very nearly went mad. I'm thirty-two and I'm unemployed and living in someone's spare room. Look at you. You've worked hard and you're very successful. You have a beautiful house, a well-paying job and a family. But you don't have any time to yourself, you never sleep and you're not happy.

CELIA: It's not about being happy. You have to be willing to make sacrifices. So I made sacrifices.

LUCY: I think it's important to be happy.

Silence.

CELIA: Look, I'm sorry. I don't mean to sound so…you know… I think your book is really good. I really do. And you've been a rock, Lucy. I've been so busy and you've been so helpful. I know we see things differently. I'm just trying to…

LUCY: To help. I know. It's ok. Don't worry about it.

16

1646. A country road. Bess speaks to a man we can't see.

BESS: All the way from London, eh? What were you doin' there? Did ye walk all this way? It true what they says 'bout the sea monster in the Thames? I heard folk down there found a great big beast of a thing lurkin' in the river. Blue 'n green scales 'n teeth 'n all. Sea monster they says. Eats cats 'n little bebbies. *Pause.* Ye ain't seen it? Well, pro'lly it's lies. Me Ma always said never trust London folk. They'll take ye fer all ye got and tell ye all sorts of tales. Folk says they been seein' all sort of peculiar things since the war started. Sea monsters in London, giants in Wales, dragons, even, up in the north. Charity Renshawe says she heard that in Westbury there's a farmer that's got a calf with two heads. He don't know what to do with it neither. Perfectly healthy little calf...only problem is it's got two heads. I saw a woman dead in a ditch not a fortnight ago. Froze to death, I reckon. A newborn babe lying still in her arms. And no one to bury them. *Pause.* Wish the war never come at all. Hardly know who yer friends are no more. Seems like everyone's took different sides. *Pause.* Lady Anne says she ain't got no need fer lady's maids now so I work in the fields. Ruined me hands, it has. I used to have beautiful, soft hands. Such lovely dresses her ladyship had. Satins and silks. Belgian lace. Ribbons. Shoes with silver buckles. All the colors of the rainbow. Always wanted a fine dress. I know satin 'n lace ain't for the likes of girls like me, but...just to have one pretty thing to wear to church, eh? Just one pretty thing. *Pause.* We've missed you. Yer ma missed you something dreadful. Thought you was dead. I waited for you, you know. 'Course there ain't no men left in Little Brideford anyhow. You look smart in your new uniform, Michael.

17

Brookfield House. 1646. Joan is speaking to Anne.

ANNE: I will not abide superstitious nonsense in my house.

JOAN: If I have a vision, it ain't ever wrong.

ANNE: A vision... You had a vision.

JOAN: I saw Cromwell's men at Brookfield House. This very day. I swear on my life, ma'am. I wouldn't lie to you.

ANNE: The Roundheads haven't been seen anywhere in the county in weeks.

JOAN: But they are coming now.

ANNE: I cannot believe it, Joan.

Joan starts to scatter herbs around the room and chants a prayer.

JOAN: May I be no man's enemy, and may I be the friend of that which is eternal and abides. May I never quarrel with those nearest me, and if I do, may I be reconciled quickly.

ANNE: What are you doing?

JOAN: A threshold blessing. And a protection spell.

ANNE: A spell?

JOAN: May I never devise evil against any man, and if any devise evil against me, may I escape uninjured and without the need of hurting him.

Bess enters, looking frightened.

BESS: My lady…

ANNE: What is it?

JOAN: May I love, seek, and attain only that which is good. May I wish for all men's happiness, and envy none.

BESS: I saw soldiers on the road.

ANNE: Soldiers?

BESS: It's Roundheads. I can tell by the uniforms.

ANNE: May god help us…

Meg enters.

JOAN: May I never rejoice in the ill fortune of one who has wronged me.

ANNE: Meg…the Roundheads. They're coming.

MEG: Lord have mercy…

JOAN: May I give all needful help to my friends, and to all who are in want.

BESS: Meg, did you—

MEG: Hush, now!

ANNE: If they know how few we are…

JOAN: May I win no victory that harms either me or my opponent.

Bess goes to the window.

BESS: They're coming closer, m'lady.

ANNE: We don't stand a chance against soldiers. We are unarmed.

MEG: What will you do, m'lady?

ANNE: There is nothing left to do. I will have to plead with them.

BESS: Will they show us mercy?

ANNE: We are merely women.

JOAN: May I never discuss who is wicked and what wicked things he has done, but know good men and follow in their footsteps.

BESS: But ma'am—after Naseby, I heard the Roundheads killed one-hundred women camp followers. Slashed their throats.

MEG: We'll die in this house if we stand against those soldiers.

ANNE: This war is as good as finished. We have no quarrel with them. All we want now is peace, an end to this violence.

JOAN: May I never fail a friend in danger. Mother of all, blessings to you, bless us. Earth beneath us, blessings to you, bless us.

MEG: We should plead for clemency, ma'am.

ANNE: They'll know this is a Royalist household. I am the widow of a Royalist officer. I don't think they will give me clemency. I'll say the rest of you are willing to be loyal to Cromwell. And I will surrender myself. I can only pray they'll be merciful.

JOAN: And what if they ain't? They're soldiers. Why should they show us mercy? Will they show me mercy? They'll torture me and hang me. I can't face it. I can't. I'll kill myself first.

Joan points to Meg.

JOAN: She's got nothing to worry about. She's the one that's given us all up.

ANNE: Meg, is this true?

MEG: Forgive me, your ladyship.

ANNE: How could you do it?

MEG: It was for my son Michael.

ANNE: Your son? But your son's dead.

MEG: He went over to Cromwell. He's all I got left, your ladyship. It was for him. I don't care about the Puritans or

Cromwell or the king. I care about my son. I'm sorry. Please forgive me.

BESS: Meg, we have to hide them. Michael will make sure we're spared. We can face the soldiers. We won't tell them where you are, ma'am.

ANNE: I cannot bear it. After all William fought for...to give up this house to those who've betrayed their own king and still call themselves Englishmen... I cannot bear it.

MEG: I'm sorry, my lady.

BESS: What about the priest hole? You could escape down below the house and into the back woods.

MEG: I'll say...I'll say you left a few days ago. On a journey, to visit relations in Devon. I'll say you were travelling with a maidservant. So's if you 'n Joan are found...

ANNE: Aye.

BESS: May God be with you.

18

PAMELA: I never did see Charlie again, but I did receive a letter that I should meet a Captain Smythe at the National Portrait Gallery. In front of the Van Dyke painting of Charles I. He asked me if I would consider a mission. It was nice. Feeling wanted. And they assured me I wouldn't have to wear a hideous uniform. That glamour was best. That the better you look, the more information you'll get out of people. Smashing, I thought. Just smashing.

And so here I am now. Five years later. In a hotel bar in Istanbul. Having a gin and tonic with an Egyptian gentleman. To the uneducated ear, we're having a casual chat about the last time we met in Budapest, although we both know we've never met in Budapest. We have to be very careful because you never know who's listening. It's nice to get away from London, from the smog and the blackouts. I wrote Charlotte a postcard this morning. Hello from Istanbul! It's awfully hot here but one does eventually get used to it, I thought as I lit a cigarette.

19

2014. London. Lucy is in her room packing. Celia enters.

Celia looks around.

LUCY: You're home early.

CELIA: I thought you were coming to the book launch.

LUCY: I wasn't feeling well.

CELIA: What are you doing?

LUCY: I thought it was time for me to go.

CELIA: But why?

LUCY: I don't want to be a burden to you.

CELIA: You're not a burden.

LUCY: I think I'm in the way and I've been here far too long. Like you said, I need to take responsibility for myself. Thank you for letting me stay, but I need to go.

CELIA: You seem upset.

LUCY: Celia...you've put me under a lot of pressure.

CELIA: I've put you under a lot of pressure?

LUCY: I stayed with you for a little while and before I knew it I was taking care of your child, doing your washing, running your errands. I haven't had a single job interview since I've been here.

CELIA: You can't blame me for that.

LUCY: You were calling me constantly. I stopped going to AA meetings because I haven't had time. Because you didn't think it was important.

CELIA: I don't think that's very fair. You know, you could have said something. If you thought I was using you.

LUCY: I didn't say that. I didn't say you were using me.

CELIA: Look, I'm sorry if you're upset, but you don't have to leave like this.

LUCY: I need to go.

CELIA: Where are you going?

LUCY: I'm not sure yet.

CELIA: What's going on?

LUCY: Celia, I didn't want to say anything, but…

CELIA: What is it?

LUCY: I think it's important to be honest with you.

CELIA: Honest about what?

LUCY: I really don't know how to say this because you're my friend. Jeremy…there have been a few times when… At first I thought, well, I know how things can be misinterpreted. And once he came home late and he'd been at the pub, I think. And I tried to ignore it.

CELIA: He tried it on with you. *Pause.* Don't look so shocked. I know what he can be like. You're not the first woman, or even the first friend of mine that he's... I've thought about leaving, but I wanted Georgina to grow up with a father. Girls who grow up without fathers always have issues with men. And it doesn't look very good, does it? Claiming to be the woman who has it all when you're in the middle of a divorce.

LUCY: What I'm trying to say is he...started getting more persistent, but I didn't know what to do and I didn't want to say anything. He came into my room one night and I was actually quite... He said I'd been teasing him...and he locked the door...

CELIA: What?

LUCY: And he...

CELIA: No.

LUCY: I mean, we didn't...but he...

CELIA: Look, if you slept with Jeremy, I mean of course I'm upset, but I'm not surprised. You're very pretty. He's always fancied you. And he's not bad looking.

LUCY: It wasn't consensual, Celia.

CELIA: I don't believe you. Jeremy would never do something like that.

LUCY: Celia, I said no but he wouldn't listen. He pinned me down and then he put one hand on my neck and the other—

CELIA: I won't listen to this. And if you keep pressing this, this story that you've clearly fabricated on me, our friendship is over.

LUCY: It was sexual assault. I needed you to know. *Pause.* I've decided not to press charges.

CELIA: Even if you did, no one would believe you.

They stare at each other. Lucy goes back to packing. Celia watches Lucy finish packing in silence. Lucy finishes. She picks up her bags.

LUCY: You've changed. We used to be such good friends. We trusted each other. I hardly recognise you anymore. *Pause.* You still have my book.

Celia takes it out of her bag.

CELIA: I have it here, actually. I was going to give it to that editor for you.

LUCY: Can I have it back please?

Celia stares at her.

LUCY: Give it to me.

Celia's phone rings. She lets it ring. The phone keeps ringing and then stops. Celia stands over the wastebasket. She takes out a lighter and holds it up to the book. Lucy grabs the book from Celia and walks out.